C0-ARS-450

386 -2
61

Social Work and Social Living

By Bertha Capen Reynolds

Learning and Teaching in the Practice of Social Work
Re-Thinking Social Case Work
Between Client and Community
An Experiment in Short Contact Interviewing

Social Work and Social Living

Explorations in Philosophy and Practice

Bertha Capen Reynolds

NASW Classics Series

National Association of Social Workers, Inc.
1425 H Street, N.W.
Washington, D.C. 20005

Copyright 1951 by Bertha Capen Reynolds

First NASW Classics Edition 1975

National Association of Social Workers, Inc.
1425 H Street, N.W.
Washington, D.C. 20005

International Standard Book Number 0-87101-071-2
Library of Congress Catalog Card No.: 75-29534
NASW Publications No.: CBC-071-C

Printed in the U.S.A. 1975

*All case stories in this book have been disguised
and any resemblance to any person., living or dead,
is purely coincidental.*

This book is dedicated to an unbreakable
tie with the interests of humanity

LIBRARY
792170   ALMA COLLEGE
ALMA, MICHIGAN

Foreword

Greeting

Why should there be a Foreword, which is, after all, written last like a postscript? It is this author's hail and farewell to the readers who have been almost visibly close during the writing of this book. Perhaps it gathers up also the sense of incompleteness with which any great task is finished. No author says all he wants to, or all he could.

The theme of this book contains the answer to whatever appeal to the reader's understanding is implied in the personal message of a Foreword. The overall theme is that life is bigger than any single expression of it, whether that be in the art of helping troubled people, or in the writing of a book. The reader's life is bigger than anything he sees on a printed page. If a book, then, says something that a reader can use in his daily life, it will be understood.

The language of this book is as nontechnical as it could be made. A note on this point may be in order, lest some reader be as disappointed as the student in a casework class who asked, "If you were to say what you have just been saying in psychiatric language, what would it be?" My answer may be just as appropriate for the puzzled reader: "Have you learned some psychiatric language in a course somewhere? How would *your* psychiatrist say it?" In other words, since there are many technical dialects, the reader who knows one is invited to make his own translation. The reader who does not can console himself by thinking that the real test of knowing a thing well enough to apply it is, first of all, to be able to say it in simple language. Between saying a thing and doing it, however, there is often a long and hard road, which I hope will be easier because we travel it in company.

About Social Living

Where did I get the title, *Social Work and Social Living?* The experience of most of us would lead to the inference that putting together the two ideas, social work and social living, poses a contrast. Perhaps we have been on the receiving end of social work, and found it governed by rules that had little relation to what we thought were normal ways to treat people. Perhaps we have been on the giving end, and have felt that we were more "professional" the more we got used to dealing with people differently from the ways which we would ourselves like to find in social living. The theme of this book is that good professional social work is tested not by its difference but by its likeness to living well, living as a social being, and that it gets its professional stamp from being practiced by people who make a special study and discipline of how to live.

This book is not written exclusively from the point of view of a professional social worker, although Chapters IV through VII deal with technical questions connected with practice in my own field of social case-

work. This book is a critical study which finds it necessary to go into the basic philosophy of social work
itself. That philosophy, it finds, is no different when
the activity happens to be skillful leadership of groups,
the casework method of helping troubled people, or a
project in community organization. Indeed, the philosophy of social work can not be separated from the
prevailing philosophy of a nation, as to how it values
people, and what importance it sets upon their welfare. When I write, therefore, it is as a person, a citizen of the United States of America in this mid-century
period, and with a very deep consciousness that social
workers are people too. A criticism of this manuscript,
"You write as if you were outside of social work" seems
to me to be well based. I hope I do. While it is easy to
write from the inside, with all the protection of a comfortable acceptance of what exists, it is much more
challenging to "stand off and look at ourselves."

When we say that we test social work against social
living, do we mean some ideal concept of social living
that exists only in our minds? The relationships among
people in our communities range from good to unbelievably bad. We find there love and understanding, and self-forgetting heroism. We also find competition and exploitation, suspicion and deceit, hatred and
scorn. We social workers have sometimes thought that
our attitudes toward people, which are developed during professional training, are so much better than many
of those which prevail in our communities that we
should be teachers of different standards of relationship rather than learners of the common misconcep-
tions. We even hope, for instance, that our understand-

ing of behaviour difficulties will influence community attitudes to the point of prevention of much of the present incidence of neuroses and delinquency.

It is true that we are developing a scientific understanding of people that should bear fruit in better relationships. This book, however, challenges us with the question whether we cannot use, more consciously than we do, our common heritage as members of communities. Although our theories may seem to us to be compounded of intelligence and pure essence of good will, they actually do come out of what we are accustomed to doing in practice. The language of our acts, how social agencies are set up, their policies and procedures, the techniques of our practice, are forces that shape the theories which we teach. Our agencies are social institutions, molded by the same contending interests in our communities that produce both the relationships which bring people together and those that drive them apart. Whatever we find in our communities, we find also in social agencies.

Social work and social living, then, instead of being in contrast, or being artificially brought together, are inextricably mixed, and inseparable. Perhaps we are quite well able to see that this is true of social work as a whole, but psychiatric social workers (of whom I am one) generally feel that our specialty is an exception. We are apt to believe that we have a certain universality and timelessness about our knowledge of people, so that what we say of them is always true, in all sorts of social situations. This book challenges that conception, for two reasons among others:

First, we who hold these ideas about people are people ourselves, shaped from babyhood by the experiences and attitudes prevailing in our communities. If we think that a year or two of professional training (marked though it is by a conscious effort to develop a "professional self") can cut off the nourishment we get, as persons, from living in society, we were never more mistaken. All the years since we learned, as babies in our cribs, how to get along socially with our world, and all the years we have been immersed in a sea of social relationships, while we thought we were making an island of different ideals in our profession, can have only one result. Our *acts* will be the acts of the total personalities we are, regardless of the theories by which we try to explain them. If there seems to be a gap between our theory of how people should be treated and how we actually do treat them, it is our deeds which are the reality which we have to face, understand and act upon.

Secondly, if we psychiatric social workers do treat people with more understanding than is usual in community life, we do not thereby remove them from the real world while we try to create one of ideal understanding for them. Children have to live with parents who are fear-ridden and irritable, and sometimes actually reject them. Harassed teachers are quite unable to give the acceptance to each individual which a child guidance clinic would like to find. Our practice is in the world of social living, whether we like it or not, and whether or not our theories correspond with it.

This Foreword, then, introduces a challenging, perhaps disturbing book. I hope it will be also a companionable book. We can face turmoil and change in our world, and deficiencies in ourselves, if we face them in the consciousness that we are all together, and that if we are to create something better for the future we must be both clear-eyed and courageous.

BERTHA C. REYNOLDS

Stoughton,
Massachusetts.
August, 1950.

Contents

Foreword

Greeting   v
About Social Living   vi

I.   Closer to People?

1. Why This Book Had to Be Written   1
2. What Do We Mean by Closer?   1
3. Chart of the Chapters to Come   11

II.   Must It Hurt to Be Helped?

1. Exploring the Question   13
2. In Social Living?   15
3. In Social Work?   25

III.   Eligible or Belonging?

1. Selecting People *In* or *Out*   35
2. Public Obligation to Those Who Belong   45
3. Comparing Concepts of Eligibility   51

IV. Members Entitled to What?

1. In a Membership Organization   53
2. Selection Among Services   59
3. A Welcome for All   62
4. One Who Hardly Felt He Belonged   68
5. One Who Didn't Conform   71

V. Don't You Spoil People?

1. Why Social Workers Fear Doing Too Much   80
2. Why the Union Feared Social Workers   85
3. Are Clients People?   89
4. A Woman Who Might Become Dependent   91
5. A Young Couple Needs Money   99

VI. Is Diagnosis an Imposition?

1. A Bit of History   107
2. Diagnosis in Short Contacts   109
3. Two Examples:
    a. A Request for Information   111
    b. A Request for a Loan   113
4. Who Makes the Diagnosis?   116
5. Diagnoses Gone Astray   118
6. Capacity and Needs Unknown   123
7. Diagnosis and Reality   129

VII. Who Hath Despised the Day of Small Things?

1. Why Study Short and Minor Services?   132
2. The Man Who Lost His Grip   135
3. Youth Seeking Guidance   151

VIII.　Whose Need and Whose Responsibility?

1. By Way of Review　　　162
2. Society in Conflict　　　164
3. Finding the Question in a Community Center　　　166
4. "We Are Responsible"　　　170
5. How Active May a Client Be?　　　171
6. Social Workers Are People Too　　　174

VIII. Whose Need
and Whose Responsibility?

1. By Need Alone 184
2. God Is in Justice 154
3. Rights and Freedom in Comparative Cultures:
The Sun Republic 170
4. How Active Moral Obligation Is
5. Social Workers Are People Too . . . .

I.   Closer to People?

1.   Why This Book Had To Be Written

Would you be interested in a job in social work closer to people? That question, full of fateful possibilities, came over the wires to me one windy evening in March in the war year of 1943. The story of the job it led to is best told in detail in Chapter IV, as part of a discussion of how social workers used their skills somewhat differently because they were working for a membership organization. It is enough to say here that the job was in a wartime joint project between a new social agency, United Seamen's Service, and a trade union, the National Maritime Union, and that it was set up to serve seamen in the Merchant Marine.

Those four years in a lifetime of practice and teaching of social work could not be dismissed as an episode, when shipping again became normal. Those years were packed with so much learning which has import for the whole of social work that a book had to be written. This book links the work with seamen to a lifetime of knowing social workers and their problems, and tries to pass on to you the different *quality* of work with people who feel that a service belongs to them because they belong.

2.   What Do We Mean by Closer?

There are two kinds of proximity to people which we shall discuss in turn, physical and personal—how to be available and how to be "next" to people in a different sense than the proximity of two pieces of coal in a bin.

Do we realize what a problem we have in social work even to be physically present where people are? The easy answer that if they want help they should come where we are is no solution. It is interesting, for instance, to think that of thousands of seamen who represented a cross section of America, both urban and rural, we seldom found one who had had experience with a social agency, except for the mass relief of the depression of the 1930's. If a social agency appropriate to his or his family's problem was suggested to him, a seaman would almost invariably react as to something to keep away from. Perhaps it is not strange that thousands of people in the United States do not know that social agencies exist, when we consider that it is only fifteen years since the first national program of public assistance began to cover systematically the rural counties as well as urban areas.

That there are other barriers, which keep people from going to social agencies of whose existence they are aware, will be discussed when we consider getting closer to people personally. There is a further aspect of being available to people with which we must be concerned:

It is not possible to do good social work without equipment. Buildings are necessary in order to meet people, facilities for administration, equipment for recreation, education, medical care, or whatever the program of the agency demands. In addition, an agency works through community contacts, influential people, other social institutions. A new agency has to gather these facilities, and win the respect and confidence of its community. Once gained, these are valued as priceless possessions. Let us take a few examples of how service to the most needful people may conflict with an agency's wish to maintain its established position:

A group agency wants to reach the children who have least in the way of opportunities. But some of these youngsters do not know how to treat a fine building. They are noisy, dirty, and disturbing to nicer children. The building may be marred, and the community angered, before the influences of the city streets on these youngsters are overcome. So it is easy to say that the agency should serve those who are ready for its opportunities, and, after a while, the boy gangs are meeting in cellars, and the agency hears of them only in reports of delinquencies.

Or, to take another instance from group work: A community center wants to offer a forum for free interchange of ideas. Perhaps it has a difficult time explaining, when some ideas expressed in a discussion of a controversial issue are disapproved by influential people, who do not think that some sides of some questions should be expressed at all. In the end, the community center may still be offering forums, but making sure that what is said is completely safe. By this time, those who really want to express opinions go elsewhere, and the social agency has lost its hoped-for function of stimulating an active interest in vital issues, and bringing together conflicting points of view for a healthy clash of ideas.

Casework agencies are in the same predicament. People who have inconvenient problems, such as those which take too much money to solve, or which point up too clearly the need for better wages or housing, find that the agency is not equipped to meet their needs and cease to come to it. Gradually, the agency is dealing with a special clientele, while the more serious problems in the community go untouched by casework services. Most agencies do not intentionally make it their policy to avoid serious social problems, but it is easy to refine one's techniques to the point where only relatively refined people can make use of them. In later chapters we shall see how emphasis upon psychological problems has tended to limit clientele of private social agencies to people who can use a service on these terms.

There is a disturbing implication in this observed tendency of social agencies to move away from the very poor and highly disadvantaged groups in the community, even though we understand why. It is the implication that these groups are a different order of beings, whose existence we can forget if we do not see them. Public assistance and the law have been bidden to take care of them, to see that their want and their delinquencies do not give the community too much trouble. We shall discuss in later chapters the enormous possibilities that lie in the public assistance program. Here we can only note that the community, through its social planning, is in effect saying, "You can't do casework with the kind of people that private social agencies have moved away from, so of course we will not give you staff and means to waste in trying." It is not surprising to find this attitude when, at the same time, in the papers and magazines and on the screen, radio and television, the following picture of life in America is presented:

Practically all the heroes and heroines of fiction and drama are white people, middle or upper class, able to have interesting experiences. A working man who works, except under exceptionally romantic circumstances, does not appear in an important role. A Negro does not appear unless he plays a submissive part, or adds so-called comedy relief. Everyone addressed by the colorful advertisements is able to take a cruise, buy a new car or house, provide a pension for his old age with which he can travel or live in a rose-covered cottage. We are so used to this that we take it for granted, and enjoy the vicarious luxury of it all. Are we, however, sometimes aware that this means that very poor people, and members of minority groups, are not really considered a part of the world that matters, and if the comfortable folk forget them, we in social work are entitled to forget them too?

How about being closer to people in the sense of being where minds can meet, and feelings be understood and even shared? Social work has undergone many changes in relation to this issue during its history. When its modern form was developing, as a better method of dealing with the poor than the harshness of the law, or the sentimentality of almsgiving, social work was more concerned with treating situations than the people who were caught in them. The people, worthy or unworthy, were *instances* of problems like unemployment, disease, drunkenness, widowhood, or deserted families. Social workers were actively interested in movements to encourage thrift, to provide better housing, milk for children, outings in the country, better medical care, and looked forward to a decreasing incidence of poverty as reforms became effective. Though personality difficulties were seen to be at the root of some of the poverty and delinquency observed, there was small hope of influencing behavior except by religious admonition, reproof or punishment.

With the new developments in psychology after World War I, social workers eagerly grasped at opportunities for more understanding, and new methods of working with people. They began to say that a person's situation was not as important as the person in it, and what it meant to him. Feelings and ideas became their stock in trade, rather than rent money, clothing for a family, or knowledge of how to organize a campaign to clean up a slum neighborhood. This emphasis on personality will be studied in the chapters which follow, but here we may note its dynamic effect on the development of social work. It is possible to give coal without knowing more about the person than that he needs it and is entitled to it. It is not possible to work with people on problems connected with their feelings without being in a relationship with them which is close enough for them to share their feelings with the professional person.

The new profession of social work was above all anxious to be scientific. For the first time it had access to a body of theory about emotions and behaviour. It learned how to use a relationship to a person professionally, and developed rules about doing so that set this relationship apart from those occurring in everyday life. The doubts which some of you have about the desirability of being closer to people stem, I know, from theories expressed in our professional literature that urge that while we must be "close" to people we should maintain the detachment necessary for a good professional job.

It is one of the purposes of the studies in this book to try to clarify what is, and is not, "professional" in this respect. We do not want to pin a professional label unintelligently upon whatever happens to be in vogue at the moment, or discard what happens to be out of fashion. We want to test our theory and practice against a wider experience than that of our professional field alone. We want to test them against ordinary living. We can also make use of the wartime experience at the Maritime Union, which, incidentally, shattered some of the protective devices which are taken for granted in the usual social agency. While we recognize that that experience in a membership organization had many features which are not applicable elsewhere, we hope that it contains suggestions which may well be useful in any type of social agency.

Did we really get closer to people in the project at the Maritime Union? At first it might seem that it was a setting peculiarly handicapped in developing relationships. The department saw large numbers of seamen for brief periods, often only once, though many did return recurrently after sea trips. It had few of the continuing ties with families which family agencies used to have when they "stood by" for many years through successive periods of illness and disaster. The caseworkers did have opportunity to know what seamen and their families found hardest in their lives, how they struggled to make ends meet, how illness wrecked cherished plans, and how distorted relationships made happiness impossible. We knew what they wanted for their children. It was of great importance to know what they were making of the resources they had, personal and social as well as material resources, and how they could use help on their present problems. The caseworkers were constantly concerned with feelings, but always in relation to social situations which urgently needed solution.

It was amazing to the social workers who went from experience in other agencies to the Maritime Union to find so little of the resistance which they had been accustomed to meet. In a few minutes seamen were telling things about themselves (even "damaging admissions") which it would have taken many interviews to work up to in most social agencies.

It is worth noting that this was not a close personal relationship. It could not be such when caseworkers dealt with fifteen or twenty emergencies a day, and when a man who returned could not always see the same person, though an effort was made to make it possible. The inference seemed to be that anybody he would see there would be working for his interests, and he would be protected in his confidences. It was the *kind of situation*, rather than the person, which protected him. We shall refer to this again in Chapters IV and VIII.

Some of the seamen discussed the barriers which kept them from going to social agencies in the community. There was, of course, the traditional "I don't want charity" which might not come from any experience with social work, but from a sturdy independence which decried the very idea of it. There were also the

notions (which possibly did connect with experiences)
that "They don't want to help you, they only put you
through an inquisition." Also, "They don't understand
seamen" and "I don't know what they are talking
about."

One factor in the situation at the Maritime Union
may be the most important clue to the lack of resistance
found there—what union membership meant to the
men. We found that necessary referrals to public assistance were almost invariably eased if we included in
the explanation of why, and of how to proceed, the
following: "Many of the social workers you will meet
there are union members too, did you know that?" We
noted that he might run into a bad one, of course, but
most of them "knew the score." Again and again a
man's tension eased as he said, "Well, I hate to apply
anyway, but I'm glad to know there are union members there." That fact seemed to create in advance a
relationship which a union member could take hold
of.

The experience at the Union was unique in another
respect. It was closer than social workers usually get
to people who are actively working, through their own
organization, to solve their problems of making a better life for themselves and their families. The Union
had at that time not only a militant program of negoti-
ating contracts specifying wages and conditions on
ships, but provided a number of other services* to
members, in addition to the joint project with
United Seamen's Service. It had a credit union bank,

* Later, these special services to members were given up, along
with the militant union program.

free counsel for foreign-born seamen on legal matters connected with their shipping and their citizenship papers, a department for handling claims for injuries, and one for administering the Union's small weekly benefit for members who were in hospitals. Its "patrolmen," boarding ships as they docked, not only collected union dues but handled, on behalf of the Union and through its entire machinery, any grievances which had arisen during the voyage. The Union enforced "rotary hiring" through its shipping hall, insuring that seamen (all of whom carried government papers stating the jobs for which they were qualified) would be hired strictly in turn, without discrimination of any sort. The Women's Auxiliary, composed of wives and mothers of seamen, visited the sick in hospitals, and took action on legislation affecting seamen and their families.

Social workers in contact with a peoples' organization of this sort were bound to change any feeling they may have had that the world would be saved by social work, organized as such. Proximity to people working on their own problems in such well-planned ways could not but enhance a caseworker's faith in the capacity of ordinary people to do a better job for themselves than anyone outside their situation could do for them.

Most of all, this experience challenged the isolation in which we have done much of our casework. Being strangers ourselves to what goes on among people whose lives are full of hardships, we have taken our clients aside for individual treatment, not knowing their usual group relationships, or those through which they might find better solutions than are possible for them to work out alone.

3. Chart of the Chapters to Come

Our analysis of the relationship between clients and social agencies, which is basic to any work we do, will be continued in the next two chapters, Chapter II, *Must It Hurt to Be Helped?* and Chapter III, *Eligible or Belonging?* They go into the philosophy of helping and being helped, and the basis of selection of whom to help.

Chapter IV, *Members Entitled to What?* introduces a series of four studies of various technical matters in social casework. Chapter IV gives a more detailed description of actual practice in the experiment of the joint wartime agency, United Seamen's Service-National Maritime Union, at the NMU hall. This description is focused upon the effect of a setting such as a membership organization on casework practice.

Chapter V, *Don't You Spoil People?* tackles the problem of giving, both of material benefits and services.

Chapter VI, *Is Diagnosis an Imposition?* is concerned with our confusion about diagnosis in social work.

Chapter VII, *Who Hath Despised the Day of Small Things?* purposes to illustrate how one uses the skills of social casework in the small services which may seem hardly important enough for the attention of trained people.

The final chapter, *Whose Need and Whose Responsibility?* returns to the philosophy of social work as a whole, and its relation to the society in which it develops. We shall find it a critical question whether society wants the people who are served by social agencies to take responsibility on their own behalf. It is an equally critical question for social workers whether we shall let the contradictory attitudes toward people which confuse our society today shape our practice, to the destruction of professional standards. Or shall we be active, ourselves, as people engaged in social living, to make one consistent whole out of our philosophy and practice?

11. Must It Hurt to Be Helped?

1. Exploring the Question

What a peculiar question! And what different answers one might get, depending on who was asked! Some of them flash out of memory in pictures:

1. A seaman sits on the edge of a chair at the desk of a personal service worker in his Union Hall. He says, "I never asked any help before, and I wouldn't now, but I just don't know anywhere else to turn. I've got to have money for the rent today, or we'll be out on the street, and my wife is sick. If it were just me alone I could manage somehow. Could you let me have a loan? I'll pay it back just as soon as I get paid." In discussing the whole problem that faces him, it may seem that rent money is not all he needs, and a social agency may be helpful. It is explained to him that there are social agencies in the community which may give service, and perhaps a little money. "No," he says, getting up to go, "I don't want anything to do with charity. Just tell me, one way or the other, whether I can have the loan, and I won't bother you any more."

It looks as if it does hurt to be helped, even from a source to which the seaman felt able to come, and with the proviso which he insists upon that it will be a loan which he will pay back. The man has to make sure that it is understood that he asks help only under the gravest necessity, and not for himself alone.

2. A woman with a partially paralyzed husband uses a loan service for emergencies which each time are very real. She has a chronic heart condition which prevents her taking factory work, and she is not trained for an office job. She does get work, but is often ill and jobs prove temporary. When her husband is earning, she is never able to put aside anything for the periods she knows will come when he is not able to earn anything. A series of emergency loans are converted on the books of the agency to grants, when it is evident that this couple can never reasonably be expected to repay them. Increasingly, however, the wife comes for further loans in emergencies which seem to be created by her own lack of planning. One can see in her a decreasing reluctance to ask, and the casework service does not stimulate her, as was hoped, to better planning and more realistic expenditures.

While it may be painful to ask for help, isn't it fairly easy to get used to it? Especially if you know what the agency can do best and emergencies occur which just fit what it can do? Why shouldn't one use a service which is offered?

3. A psychiatrist sums up his opinion of clients of social agencies: "If there wasn't something

wrong with them they wouldn't go to an agency. Plenty of people have troubles and get out of them by themselves. I'd say every agency needs a psychiatrist, and most of what agencies do to help people is wasted time."

Does it hurt to be helped, then? The psychiatrist's reply might be: "Not if you are too far gone to care whether you are normal or not. A really normal person wouldn't want to be mixed up with social agencies."

4. A lawyer sits next to a social worker at a luncheon meeting on community welfare planning. He disagrees with what she says about making services easily available to people. "I don't believe in that. Some people take care of themselves and pay heavy taxes to make things easy for others who won't work. You ought to see the trouble I have getting anybody to mow my lawn. It ought to be so hard to get relief that nobody would try it who didn't really have to."

This reply has a musty flavor, but probably grew right here in America this year. To paraphrase: If it doesn't hurt to be helped, it should. Social agencies must *make* it hurt, or forfeit the respect of their supporters who are examples of thrift and heavy taxpaying.

2. In Social Living?

When one steps out of the role of a social worker, and out of contact with organized social agencies which are giving help, these various answers become even more confusing. What is wrong about asking for a loan at a place where one is known? Is there something about receiving help that is habit-forming, and hence to be dreaded? Is it a mark of abnormality to think of asking for it? Is seeking help shameful, and quite unfair to the people who manage by themselves?

Outside of social work, however, people seem to look upon taking and giving help as they do any other activity of life. Some people want too much help and are disciplined for it by the spontaneous reactions of those who resent it. "Pull your own sled and don't be a cry-baby." "I'm too busy. You'll have to get along as best you can." There is perhaps a greater sense of abnormality attached to being unusually averse to taking help. "I don't know what is the matter with Susan that she won't let anyone help her." "It's embarrassing to try to do anything for the Joneses. They either fall all over themselves to try to pay you back, or get their feelings hurt because you even offered." Whether it is in a country district where the word "neighbor" has more meaning than just living near, and connotes someone with whom to exchange surpluses and kindly services, or whether it is in a city where the population is settled enough to constitute a neighborhood, the person who won't share, both giving and receiving, is the queer one, the recluse. It seems that by neighborhood standards giving and taking are as normal as breathing in and breathing out.

The foregoing observations are varying in their applicability, their validity being affected, undoubtedly, by the prevailing culture and the economic status of the people concerned . A highly competitive society which gives the greatest rewards to those who are the most single-minded in pursuit of profit may mark as weakness any generosity (except to one's friends and one's inferiors), and put the badge of shame on being a recipient instead of in a position to give. Middle-class people are closer to these cultural pressures than are industrial workers whose employment is interdependent with that of many others, with whom they learn to cooperate because they can not succeed alone. Rural people, although not used to large aggregations of workers, do find family and neighborhood cooperation essential to living. What we have said about neighborly giving and taking seems, then, to be most true among working people, and least taken for granted among the well-to-do and middle-class sections of the population.

There are certain variations in attitudes about giving and receiving, dependent upon age and condition. Children, of course, are expected to be helpless in infancy, and to outgrow that state. How fast they are pushed to do for themselves and others depends on how hard the family itself is pushed by circumstances, and how much opportunity there is for a child to be useful in the family's way of earning a living. On a farm, there are little tasks at which children can be set early. I am told that some European peasants measure a child's age, not by years but by what he can do. One is old enough to feed chickens, another to harness a horse. In cities, where both parents may have factory jobs, children's usefulness may have little transition between keeping out from under foot and being given a great deal of responsibility for other children, the housework, finding kindling and earning money at odd jobs. Much of what we call adolescent rebellion is an uneven development of the ability to do without help, as compared with a desire for it which sometimes lingers to compensate for early deprivations. When financial dependence of adolescents is prolonged, as it often is in our culture, that period may co-exist with a stage of development in which the adolescent wants no part of parental advice in his affairs.

In the declining years of life, the direction of change is reversed, as help from others becomes more and more necessary. Some old people accept help increasingly, as a matter of course, and others rebel at losing their independence. The increasing pressures upon men and women in the wage-earning years, plus the shortening of the work life until old age, in the employment market, begins at forty or forty-five, makes heavy indeed the burden of caring for old people at the same time that children must be given a start in life. The answer to which many countries are moving and to which the United States is beginning to pay attention is social insurance. Family allowances and old age security would make it possible for each age group to do its own living without being a drain on the resources of any other. Community acceptance of the idea of help from others is, therefore, advancing toward a sharing of the burden that helping may entail so that all can benefit and none need be destroyed by it. The logic of the matter is that if some measure of helplessness is a concomitant of the beginning and end of life for everyone, provision for this hazard should not be left to the accident of having relatives able to produce enough to give the care needed.

Sickness, or other physical or mental disability, constitutes a normal reason for taking help, and as normal an argument for social insurance. The insurance principle has faltered, however, before the possibility that illness might consciously or unconsciously be prolonged by the pleasantness of having one's needs met without effort. It is easier to get compensation for accidents which produce visible loss of limb than for less easily measured disabilities. The whole problem of street begging which is associated with mutilations gives eloquent testimony to our tradition that able-bodied people should not ask for help from strangers, but that crippled and disabled people have a claim on anyone who sees their plight. The fact that many of them do make a profitable living by begging, or selling some trifling object on the street, may also indicate that many who give to them have a touch of superstition that a similar fate might best be warded off from themselves by getting a bit of a good deed to their credit.

Social insurance to cover the hazards of illness, however, could logically reduce the burden of disability on the community rather than to increase it. Social workers are well aware that financial anxiety, for instance, generated in both patient and family by an illness, often delays instead of hastening recovery. On the one hand, normal time for convalescence cannot be taken when loss of income is daily becoming more tragic. On the other hand, need for time to recuperate, the sense of pain and weakness in conflict with fear of being thought lazy, creates a situation in which the patient sometimes has to establish his right to depend on others by an unconscious clinging to his symptoms. How else can one be sure of being taken care of a little longer?

We have been trying to map the limits within which

it is normal to seek and give help, social insurance being, at the present time, only a fragmentary answer to
the need for dependence on relatives and friends. There
is a recognized need for dependence in childhood and
old age, and in cases of sickness or disability. Among
adults of normal health and approximately equal resources with those around them, help seems to be on
a give-and-take basis. There is a growing awareness,
along with that of a need for social insurance, that a
"normal" standard of living should include not only a
little margin for one's own emergencies, but a little surplus to share in case of emergency among friends and
neighbors. In such circumstances, taking help with the
spoken or implied promise, "I'll do as much for you
some day" is a reasonably realistic and self-respecting
social activity.

Aren't there, then, circumstances in which it does
hurt to be helped by relatives, friends or neighbors?
We have hinted at some which are embedded in our
culture, which place the responsibility for providing the
necessities of living on the biological family, and label
as failure inability, for any reason, to carry that responsibility. This tradition is an example of a "cultural lag"
in assuming that any individual can find, if he will, an
opportunity to make a good living and to save for
emergencies and for old age. This is far from being the
case in a machine age, when technical improvements
constantly eat away at the requirements for human
labor in production. Recurring economic depressions
have taught us that individuals and families cannot
cope with widespread loss of income when jobs are not
available, but we have not yet, to any adequate degree,
accepted the principle of equally widespread sharing

of the burden, either on the basis of insurance or of an unquestioned right to relief from a unit of government. Of the right to relief we shall speak in a later chapter. Here we are concerned with what we can learn about the reactions of people who are outside the range of assistance from public or private social agencies. How do they feel about being helped, and under what circumstances does it really hurt?

Relatively unimportant, but not to be ignored, are instances which arouse a fear of being made to look foolish. To give a few examples:

> A woman with a large suitcase is accosted a block from a city railroad station by a man without a porter's badge who says, "Carry your suitcase, lady?" She wants help, and wants to pay for it, but sees no identified porter. Is this a person doing a kind deed, or a crook who will disappear with her baggage? If she gives up the suitcase and he proves honest, will she be uncomfortable about being obligated to a stranger, or uncertain whether he will feel insulted if she offers to pay? If she loses her suitcase, will she be laughed at for her lack of foresight? She may end by straining her back because it is too painful to face these uncertainties about what is really meant by the offer.

The nursery rhyme about Simple Simon is a folk saying about the foolishness of asking for something that one cannot pay for. People equally dislike ambiguous offers of help which may create an obligation that the person helped cannot exactly foresee but which it may be embarrassing to meet.

Some swindles are cleverly disguised as offers of help.

To be sure, the buyer should know enough to beware when a business concern seems to be unbelievably generous, but in our modern world people are conditioned to believe that for a limited time an offer may be made in an advertising campaign which is of great advantage to the buyer who acts quickly. Since he badly needs that car, or lot of land, or cash prize to pay his debts, he signs on the dotted line, and learns later just how generous the offer was. A few such experiences make a person wary of help that looks a little too good to be true.

It hurts to be helped when one is not in a position to repay. Among friends, the repayment may not be immediate nor to the same person, even, but the possibility and the will to do as much must be felt. If kindnesses are done among all the members of a group, each one feels the psychological "insurance" of his share in the general good will. Fraternal orders are built on this principle, and this mutual exchange of services goes on informally in neighborhoods everywhere. A woman who had every reason to move away from a city district in which she had had a most devastating experience said one day, "But I don't dare. What if my family were sick or my husband lost his job?" In that particular foreign-language community she could count on credit at the small stores, and help in sickness, which she feared would be completely lacking in the country place to which she longed to take her children. She belonged here, and could not look forward to belonging in like manner anywhere else.

The need to repay is strongly characteristic of merchant seamen whose extremely hazardous occupation produces frequent emergencies, and whose financial resources may be tied up in a wage dispute or in litigation over an injury claim. They have been accustomed to borrowing from each other, and to getting credit (at high cost) in waterfront stores. During the war, when these sources dried up, and a Personal Service was organized to help them in emergencies, they would not even consider financial aid except as loans which it was their code to repay scrupulously whenever their circumstances permitted. Social workers who dealt with them often saw that a grant, rather than a loan, was indicated when serious disability or a large family made it doubtful if a seaman could repay. At the suggestion, however, many a man walked out with a "Thank you, but I don't want charity," when all that stood between him and hunger and cold was the slim chance of meeting a seaman friend.

We have spoken of the rebellion of some old people against being unable to do for themselves. Aside from concern over the struggle to live which their sons and daughters are having (and in which the old person's care is really felt as a burden whether or not there is actual complaint about it), there is bitterness for many over the gradual slipping away of the strength and abilities they once had. The ability to be useful in old age in ways that are different from, but no less valuable than, the contributions to society in earlier years is realized by comparatively few old people. What they can give in wisdom and affection in their increased leisure often seems not to be wanted. Perhaps the most bitter experience of all is to feel left over from a former world, from which old friends are gone, and to be an unwanted tenant of a new world in which everyone's ideas and interests are incomprehensible, so that one has nothing to give.

That which is painful in old age—not belonging and hence not being able to give, while one must take from others—is a very real hurt that anyone may feel over being helped. Why is it that children can take, and give, so normally in a happy family? Is it not that they feel they belong? Why is it that some children are terribly disturbed about what they receive from their parents? Child guidance clinics find the answer in evidences of rejection underneath what some of these parents give to their children, as well as in what they withhold. Many foster children make unceasing efforts to convince themselves that they really *belong* somewhere, and vary in their reactions to the foster home from being unable to take what good things it offers to being exorbitant in their demands for more. Sick people often revert to childhood in their reactions to receiving care, and can be comfortable about it only so long as they feel that their sickness genuinely entitles them to belong, as patients, to those who care for them. Once they feel that they do *not* belong, that their diagnosis is not right for this hospital, or their convalescence is too far advanced for the kind of treatment they have been receiving, signs of strain appear. They become, perhaps, more demanding and irritable, perhaps guilty and restless. Perhaps they even revert to old symptoms to bring back the unquestioned right to be cared for because they belong here.

We have been exploring the meaning of taking help in ordinary social living. It does not seem to be painful to most people if there are certain conditions surrounding the source of help and the need for it. It is not hard to take help in a circle in which one feels sure of belonging. Indeed, the offer of help may be just the reassurance of his place in the group that a person in trouble needs. It is not hard if one has a reasonable hope of being able to contribute to the group again. It hurts to be helped when one is thereby relegated to the status of a child or permanently handicapped person. It hurts to feel that one will be expected to pay for the help in some way which he would not choose, or perhaps can not even foresee. It hurts to feel doubtful of being able to repay at all, and by that means to be again in full status as a giving, as well as receiving, member of the group.

3.   In Social Work?

After becoming used to the naturalness of taking and giving help in ordinary living, it is something of a shock to turn back to organized social work, and to find to what a large extent the reverse is true. Why?

One answer, perhaps too obvious, is that we have a hang-over from the bad old days of a harsh and degrading charity. People who took help should be made to feel outside the normal group, or they would be endlessly demanding. They should not have a status as desirable as that of people who gave—or at least were able to meet their own needs. This attitude is far from dead in our present culture, as those who have fought for adequate standards of public assistance well know. The lawyer at the luncheon meeting speaks again: "I don't believe that social services should be easily available to people."

Modern social work, however, has liked to think that it is very different. We have a whole new vocabulary in which the worth and dignity and self-determination of the client figure prominently. Why should anyone object to being helped if he meets in an agency this kind of attitude? Has organized social work traveled so far from the condescending philanthropy which we decry that resistance to it is just an indication that the client has an emotional problem, or that he is a victim of attitudes in the community that ought to have died, but certainly have not been buried?

However resistance originates, it is one of the facts of life in social work. Students in this new profession are taught how to deal with it. Professional literature has grown up around it. The psychological concept of ambivalence has been used to explain the resistance which is commonly observed. People both want help and do not want it, so runs the theory, and they cannot move in the direction of voluntarily taking and using help unless they can be brought to recognize and deal with their resistance to taking it. Perhaps their resistance is even an overcompensation for an excessive desire for help, which they must also face. It is assumed that these resistances also play a part in receiving help under the conditions of ordinary social living.

All this may be true, and for reasons that go deep into the psychological forces operating in human beings. What concerns us here is whether, since resistance is more marked in relation to social agencies than in the give-and-take of everyday life, there is something in the way social agencies are administered that creates resistance to taking help from them. How do agencies rate when we apply to them the criteria we have used in relation to the acceptability of receiving, in social living?

1. The criterion of belonging. We shall explore this further in Chapter III, but we are immediately struck by the fact that social agencies are not, generally speaking, membership organizations in which those who use the services have a major voice. Voluntary social agencies, at least, represent someone doing for someone else. Can any amount of explanation or courteous treatment make the person helped feel that the service belongs to him? Without giving a categorical answer regarding our theory, it is certain that our practice is far from reaching a solution.

2. The criterion of keeping full adult status while receiving help. We have seen that in our culture adult status demands reciprocal giving and taking within a natural group. Feeling at home in a group which offers help requires that full status shall not be denied in other ways. For a large number of people in our society, discrimination on account of race, creed, color, national origin or political belief is a bitter reality. A Negro who is not considered good enough to vote, to have his word taken as a witness in court, or to serve on juries, cannot take help from an agency which represents that society to him, and feel that he has not suffered further impairment of his status as a man. The counsel he receives is weighted with the condescension with which society regards him, no matter how fine a human being his individual case worker may be.

It is appalling to think that society not only places minority groups outside its full acceptance, but that it creates a disadvantaged group out of the very fact of receiving help. The client's honesty may be questioned beyond the necessity of establishing facts. His judgment is not considered valid. Perhaps he is given voucher relief instead of cash, implying that he cannot be trusted to spend money given him. The newspapers rave about relief clients not being sufficiently supervised in the spending of their dole, nor even in their private lives. Private social agencies used to try to keep "worthy" families from having to become recipients of public aid which would carry a "stigma." During the depression of the 1930's, thousands of families found themselves declassed from being fully accepted members of society to the status of wards of the community, grudgingly supported and dictated to as children or mentally deficient adults might be. The suddenness with which this came about, through the one circumstance of being laid off of a job, awakened many people to the absurdity of class distinctions based, more than they had realized, on the chance that one has access to an adequate income. This need not be earned, so it became apparent, since dividends might go on when wages did not; but not to have to take help was somehow the requisite mark of full membership in the community.

> 3. The criterion of having a recognized capacity to repay, at some time and in some way. This is closely related to the maintenance of adult status in a natural group, for taking from strangers may make it obvious that one will have no opportunity to repay. There is also the urgency of feeling as capable as those who give help. Sickness and misfortune may "get me down" temporarily, so thinks

the person who is aided, but the same may happen to others whom I can help when I am on my feet again. Those who are really permanently handicapped have no small problem of adjustment around this very question of what they can give back. As our social work practice has become increasingly sensitive to this basic need, rehabilitation workers have tried to develop in every possible way the patient's ability to do something useful for others. Those too sick to be able to do anything have been cheered by being reminded how much they have already given. The administration of social agencies has too frequently, however, felt that the agency was generous in making people feel that they were welcome to its service, without any provision for their need to repay to be satisfied. Agencies have preferred not to give loans which clients asked for (and there are, of course, great difficulties in administering them and distinguishing service from business loans). They have felt that to fall in with the client's hope that he could repay was to be too optimistic, and not to help him "face reality." Under these circumstances is there reassurance in an agency's reiteration that it is glad to be of service?

4. The criterion that help must be what it looks to be, without strings attached. We have noted before that most people have reason to be suspicious of benefits offered on no reciprocal basis, and for no apparent reason. There is much suspicion of free medical treatment, even today, on the ground that "They only want to experiment on people who can't

pay." What social workers might want to gain is perhaps too vague a concept to be stated as clearly as this, but the very uncertainty is terrifying. "She told me I'd have to change before I could get anything from them. I told her to keep it." Social workers do have some desires of their own for a satisfying form of professional experience, and perhaps agencies have also their own reasons for being which bring their own rewards. How does it look, however, to the person on the other side of the desk?

The question whether social agencies create some of the resistances they encounter when help is offered has not been answered, and perhaps cannot be. Social work is an inseparable part of the community, and the society in which it grows may itself throw up barriers to social service which the best casework practice cannot overcome. Our method of studying such questions is to observe the circumstances in which giving and taking help are most natural, even in a competitive society, and then to see how far it is possible for the administration of social agencies to reproduce these natural conditions. Much research, with careful checking of data, should go into what is here only a review of immediately available experience, to see what suggestions for study it holds for us.

To create natural conditions, however, is not necessarily enough for a profesional service in the giving of help. When medical social service began to be developed in hospitals, it was thought of as *putting back* into the care of the patient in a large institution what had been lost with the disappearance of the good old family friend, the country doctor. Medical social service became more than that, however. Just as modern laboratories and well-trained specialists could give a better chance of recovery to patients than the poorly equipped doctor working alone could give, so trained social service could be vastly more reliable in its helpfulness than the well-intentioned, but often inept, help of neighbors.

In becoming professional, social work should be able to mark an advance in every respect from the aid that people can get informally from friends and neighbors. A belief that this advance can be demonstrated to our public has given us confidence to talk about charging fees to clients able to pay—fees for something we are sure is good.

Must it hurt to be helped professionally, even if it does not hurt to make use of unskilled service? It is disturbing to find that an influential body of thought, expressed in professional literature and in practice, makes pain an essential concomitant of the helping process. Why "disturbing," if it is a fact? It does set up, of course, a handicap we had not counted on in establishing a demand for our professional services. We are inviting people to suffer for an ultimate improvement which we see better than they, while all around them are opportunities for unprofessional help which is relatively easy to take and seems quite natural. We have probably never faced the extent of the competition to our services, not only from friends and neighbors of clients, but from services offered by membership organizations, trade unions, political clubs, and fraternal orders. Can we prove to our communities that professional service is enough better than unskilled helping to justify giving it with some infliction of suffering?

Suppose, on the other hand, that it is not a fact that taking help is necessarily painful in order to achieve a lasting and really beneficial result. It then becomes urgent for us to know whether social agencies are producing community attitudes about using their services which create a barrier against those who need such help. It becomes urgent for the future of social agencies themselves to know whether they are sacrificing to a theory, which may not be valid, an opportunity for a wider acceptance and larger usefulness in their community.

What theoretical basis is there for the belief of social workers that taking professional help is necessarily a painful process? The idea that it is links closely, in professional literature, with a philosophy of individual self-sufficiency, and an assumption of individual failure. The person in trouble is supposed to feel shame that he has not solved his problem himself, and to show reluctance to accept help from a source outside his own circle of relatives and friends. Social workers are taught to recognize this painful feeling by some such statement as, "It must have been hard for you to come here," and to deal with the resistance they encounter with the understanding that it may be due to resentment against the circumstances which forced the client to come.

In addition, some of the current theories of social casework associate fear of change with the painfulness of taking help. Professional service, they believe, can only be used if the person asking it is willing to change his own ways of solving his problems which he must be prepared to admit have failed. He must cooperate with the agency in accepting its controls, in use of time for instance, and in ways of approaching his problem.

He must move along with the agency, or it cannot help him. An agency which is oriented to this group of theories may find that a large number of applicants drop out, because they fear change in themselves too much, or are too well satisfied with their own way of solving their difficulties. These the agency would not consider good objects of agency effort. The applicants who remain may find it painful to take help, but they will have demonstrated their willingness to change, and can be given a much more curative experience than would otherwise be possible. These theories isolate the professional giving and taking of help as a special situation, different from anything in ordinary life, and postulate that there is a different psychology of the helper and the person being helped, because of a dissimilar relationship to the social agency, which sets the limits of the help which can be offered, and the methods of giving it.

The explorations in this chapter have not been based upon the same assumptions, nor have they reached the same conclusions as the foregoing theories. We know that individual and family self-sufficiency is not possible in a machine age. The stigma of having failed to be self-sufficient is a favorite brand which those who hate social work put upon the recipients of any benefits from it. Unfortunately, many people of the middle class from which most social workers have come have unthinkingly adopted the same idea that anyone (except an incompetent) can succeed if he will. If he fails—so runs the prevailing opinion fostered by our press and radio—the trouble must be in himself, and he must be induced to change by an agency better equipped than he to lay down the rules of the game of life.

Our study of social living in its historical perspective, and in the dynamic struggle for human survival which goes on today, reveals above all else the interdependence of modern society, and the impossibility of a purely personal success or failure. There is no ground for assuming that clients of social agencies have necessarily failed when such a basic need as an opportunity to earn a living is no longer in individual hands, and when wretched housing, ill health and frustration take a terrible toll from family life. These studies point to the conclusion that recognition of what a client has to work with, in himself, is a better starting point than an attempt to make him accept his failure, and that building him up as a person makes him more ready, rather than less so, to go on to further growth and accomplishment. It is not on record that recognition and upbuilding are painful experiences to endure.

May there be, however, something in the way that social agencies are set up, especially in the requirements they make for admission, that constitutes a barrier between people in need and their use of professional services? We shall consider this question in the next chapter.

III. Eligible or Belonging?

1. Selecting People *In* or *Out*

We have been reviewing attitudes toward the taking of help as if the kind of help did not make much difference. Are there not real differences in the way people feel about taking money, for example, as compared with opportunities for education of jobs? Services, like recreation or medical care, which cost money are traditionally not as hard to take as money itself. These differences are real, and go back to attitudes having deep roots in our society; but the differences seem to be more in degree than in absolute quality. We have found maintenance of self-esteem and of a sense of belonging to be of primary importance, and the various kinds of help, material aid, physical care, opportunities, or counsel differ chiefly in the effect they have upon this fundamental necessity.

There is a difference, however, when seeking help is voluntary, that is, the person is free to choose whether to ask for it or to do without it, as distinguished from being driven to take it by inescapable need. The lengths to which some people will go in endurance of privation rather than ask help is a measure of the social stigma which they feel. Need of money and physical care are most often associated with extremely painful necessity. Opportunities to work can be sought with a sense of returning something of one's own. Other kinds of opportunity, and counsel, not being as essential to survival usually, are more open to choice whether to seek them or not. The degree of choice seems to have a definite relationship to the possibility of taking help without loss of self-esteem.

The history of social work is full of examples of agencies for assistance which, because of their control over the necessities of life, were able to offer what looked like a choice of other services. Relief to destitute people might be accompanied by prayer and Bible reading, by inculcation of thrift, temperance pledges, attendance at clinics, which, though supposed to be benefits in themselves, were as much conditions for receiving help as were requirements of signs of improvement in cleanliness and morals. The poor were not exactly free to refuse these, though undoubtedly they found unheralded ways to make it hard for their reformers to see very satisfactory results from their labors.

The assumption back of these offerings of unasked-for benefits seems to have been that what was given was good (for the community certainly, and for the individual if he were only able to see it). Since the means of "doing good" were not unlimited, however, some selection of those who should receive benefits had to be made. It was not a question of who would choose to be helped, but of who was worthy to be chosen, out of the many necessitous folk who were always on the margins of society. Worthiness to receive necessities like food and warmth was quite simply related to the willingness of the recipients to take the other services which were tied in to the same package.

There was a period, earlier than that of the charity organization movement, when benevolence was unselective because it was other-worldly in its motives. Giving alms was good for the souls of the givers, no matter what its effect on those who received. Or, to turn to another motive, placing a crèche at the door of a convent, so that unwanted infants could be deposited there to be reared by the church, was for the purpose of saving precious souls.

Consideration of the effect of indiscriminate giving on the problems of poverty and illegitimacy came later, and was an advance in a social responsibility oriented to this present world. Being responsible in giving seemed to mean putting effort and material aid where it would yield the most good for society. The interpretation of social good has varied greatly through the years. How does it look to us who live in an age which we like to think of as "modern" and scientific, separated from the philanthropy of the 19th and earlier centuries by a wide and deep gulf?

The first thing that strikes us is that private social agencies adapt their programs to the sources and availability of their funds. Since they cannot help everybody, how shall they insure that funds contributed shall be used to the best advantage? Voluntary giving (by social agencies) carries the implication of voluntarily ceasing to give, as well. The funds for private social agencies can only be stabilized on the basis of a campaign already conducted, so that budgets can be allocated for the coming year. A disaster, or an economic depression which increases need, faces a private agency with a deficit unless it has reserve funds which it is willing to use in just such emergencies. Inflationary prices have, of course, the same effect as a disaster. It is usual for private agencies in such a situation to place the burden of the deficit on their clientele, and their staff, and to distribute the curtailment of service through some form of restriction of intake. Private social agencies have, then, both a normal process of selection for the best use of their resources, and, periodically, a sharpened intake policy to cut services to fit their funds.

What possible methods of selection of clients are open to private social agencies? Most of them have some roughly marked area of operation, such as assistance to families, placement of children, scholarships for able students, pensions for old people. Sometimes eligibility for benefits is limited by the terms of an endowment to, for instance, orphans of members of certain religious bodies, Scotch widows, indigent musicians. When, however, it comes to selection on a case-by-case basis, there are three criteria, or combinations of them, which are related to the best expenditure of funds. We might name them, (1) the value of the applicant to society, (2) the likelihood of success in carrying out the purposes of the agency, (3) research interest in the case. Suppose we think about them in turn:

1. The value of an applicant to society. What assumptions lie behind the concept that a social agency selects cases which best repay society for the help given to them? Inevitably, the agency which chooses becomes the judge of value. It may do this impersonally, selecting according to some

formula such as families with young children, or those who have never had agency help before. During the period after the establishment of public assistance, when private agencies still raised much of their money on the basis of a relief-giving function, they chose among applicants for relief, assuming that public aid would take care of the general run of cases, but that certain ones had some special reason for different treatment. A New York subway advertisement for private family agencies, a few years ago, based its appeal for funds on saving worthwhile people from having to go to public relief. The advertisement was protested on the ground that it was an insult to public relief applicants, as well as an unsound principle of selection. It seems that the terms have changed, but the same coinage of ideas persists from the period when we heard about "the worthy poor." Now the criterion by agency standards is that people have good standards, high intelligence and ability, are able to make something of themselves.

2. The expectation of successful treatment is closely related to, but not identical with, the criterion of value to society. A social agency may feel quite free not to ask, for instance, whether an invalid whom it helps to a better adjustment will give very much to the world. It may be willing to let a client be the judge of the value of its service to him, provided that he wants help enough to meet the conditions which predict success of the agency's chosen form of treatment. The test of "worthiness" to echo the old word, would then be

willingness to cooperate, "ability to use our service," to show desired changes in behavior or a better adjustment of life conditions. By this method of selection, the agency chooses those who want its offered service, and tests the strength of that desire.

3.   Research is generally accepted as a valid way of benefiting society by improving service in the long run. Social work has advanced so little in organized research that it is usually in association with other professions, such as medicine and psychology, that it uses the criterion of research interest for selection of cases. A private agency may select cases of certain types of problem, or certain personality difficulties, so that study of large numbers of these may yield data of social value. Once the selection for research interest is made, the treatment of the client's need may be genuinely the best that the agency knows how to give.

The critical difficulty facing all agencies which select cases is that, once they have set up norms for what they want, tests must be devised to give some reliable indication of who conforms to the norm. Once selection has proceeded from the simpler criteria of age, sex, residence, to the type of problem presented, or the expectation of success, tests are of extraordinary difficulty.

For one thing, if selection is by type of problem, what is presented may not be what is really troubling the person. Psychological studies have made us aware that people disguise what they cannot bear to face, under a less painful request which they sense will be acceptable. To begin with that request, and to help the person to move from that to his real need, of which he may not even be conscious at first, is a diagnostic service which is essential if an agency is to know the problems with which it is dealing. To test the applicant by his disguised request, and send him elsewhere, perhaps before he has clarified his need, is to lose the very basis of a sound decision.

Social agencies which select cases by type of problem on the basis of one interview have a firm belief in their interviewing methods. They assume that an applicant can be gotten quickly into rapport with the caseworker, so that he is, practically from the start, in full command of himself, and able to show all his assets and liabilities for inventory. In our experience that is seldom the case, especially when the factor of being tested is a definite part of the situation. No matter how skillfully questions are disguised, the person knows, not necessarily what the requirements are, but that somehow he is being judged. The identification of the real problem, and the testing of an individual's ability to cope with it, require more time, and more commitment by the agency to sharing in the difficulties, than many agencies are willing to invest.

The test of likelihood of success in casework has been clarified as agencies have come to define their function more precisely. A school of thought has grown up in social work around the concept that agency function is determinative of what can be done in case treatment. The applicant's ability to define his problem, so as to see if it conforms to the function of the agency to which he has come, and his acceptance of the agency's limitations and the conditions it sets, as well as the benefits it offers, are the preconditions for service. Under such a system of selection, an agency can count on a high percentage of successful cases.

Definition of an agency's function is undoubtedly an advance in the growth of social work into a profession. It marks a step forward from a diffuse taking on of all the problems which could be found lying about in any person's life. We have come to expect, however, in modern social work, that there will be some over-all community planning to meet social needs, in place of the *laissez-faire* selection by agencies of clients which interest them, letting the devil (to speak irreverently) take the hindmost clients who interest nobody. While it sounds valid for private agencies to do what they are equipped to do best, a community may well ask whether it supports agencies to meet need, or to express themselves. In other words, the value of voluntary social agencies to a community is in their being able to follow a changing pattern of community needs flexibly, and as completely as possible, and to change functions rather than to maintain them rigidly in face of changing needs. According to this conception, therefore, when an agency asks a client to measure himself and his problem against its stated function, it cannot discharge its responsibility just by saying that he does not fit, or that some other agency should accept him. That is not the same as saying that any other agency can or will accept him, nor is it the same as saying that a careful search reveals that no resource exists in the community for this particular need. It is also not the same as taking responsibility to awaken a community to such instances of unmet need.

Selection of cases by the criterion of an anticipated success in treatment presents other difficulties than that of how to discharge responsibility to the community for those not accepted. Success may be predicated upon factors which are complex and baffling. Are those chosen, perhaps, the most verbal among a large number who have the same problems? Are they the most intelligent? Should the selection be frankly stated as a choice by intelligence? Are those who conform most completely to the agency's requirements a submissive group, not strong in ego development and willing to pay any price asked for being helped? Or are they, on the contrary, expected to be so sure of themselves and of what they want that the most needful applicants are sifted out? Does an agency which emphasizes the theory that taking help is inherently a painful process thereby select applicants who have a large component of masochism in their personality, which responds to caseworkers whose own needs may have led to their selection of this particular approach to casework practice? These questions could only be aswered by more thorough research than we have yet seen undertaken in social work. They are asked here only to illustrate the complexity of any method of selection for the services of a community agency, through an attempt to appraise the worth of an individual to society, or by testing conformity to an agency's methods of work, on the assumption that the resulting success in treatment guarantees that the agency has rendered service of the greatest value.

Selection by an agency of those who are to receive its benefits, however necessary the process may be to keep service realistic in relation to funds and the use of the agency staff, is not a comfortable concept to live with, philosophically. If the agency's services are not vitally needed it is assumed that the community would not raise money to supply them. If they are necessary, and especially if they involve supplying the essentials of subsistence, why should any one individual or group have such control over others as to decide whether these others shall actually live or die? How can an agency with limited funds, which has to make such decisions on the basis of its means, take such a responsibility for human lives? When an agency which is an arm of government which has taxing power takes responsibility for supplying the necessities of life, it is at least subject to appeal, and can be reached by public pressure and legislative action in a democracy.

The burden of denial of necessities to people who had no other resource has forced agencies, throughout the history of social work, to find some reason for refusing aid that would put the responsibility on the applicant. He must be found not worthy, or not cooperative, or the existence of his need must in some way be denied. Much of the harshness with which "charity" has traditionally been associated has been due to an attempt to deal with an impossible situation. Administrators of limited relief funds have been placed in the position of having to sweep back a tide of human misery with little brooms. To survive, they had to steel themselves to believe, as the sponsors of charities did also, that there was work for everyone who would bestir himself to find it, and only bad personal habits and stubborn ignorance prevented people from taking advantage of advice that would have solved their problems. The religious tradition which has always been strong in social work fostered a belief in unlimited resources, spiritual if not material. Social workers said, and meant it, "No worthy person shall go away from our door unhelped. God will provide the means if we only have faith." They did not see that this created a temptation to hold their comfortable faith at the expense of the needy person who, they decided, was unworthy.

It has been hard for social workers to place themselves under a scientific discipline, and to face the fact that as far as they are concerned, money and strength come to an end. Private social agencies do have to refuse people at some point, and without reference to their merit or the validity of their need. Only if an agency offers services which, though desirable, are not necessary for survival, can it escape the dilemma of either usurping a function of government in using power to control the lives of human beings, or of placing upon the applicants for aid an unrealistic expectation that they can, if they will, always secure the necessities of life for themselves.

2. Public Obligation to Those Who Belong

It was inevitable that the whole people of the United States, through their representative government, should at some point have to take the responsibility for seeing that the necessities of life were available to all. An economic depression, in a long line of depressions, but unprecedented in severity and duration, forced government to take that responsibility in the 1930's. At that time the word *eligibility* came into the vocabulary of social work with entirely new meaning.

Under the structure of public assistance which was hammered out during the crisis years of that decade, eligibility came to mean proof of need, as defined by law. Merit in one's personal life was irrelevant, in the sense that conduct unbecoming a citizen could be dealt with by law otherwise, but need for subsistence was just as much the responsibility of government in a democracy as, for instance, education for good citizenship. Experience in the depression highlighted the absurdity of trying to teach in free public schools children who were too hungry to learn, or trying to keep people out of heated jails who were perishing with cold as "good" citizens.

Another concept was inseparable from that of proof of need in the definition of eligibility, the concept of belonging. Every relief investigation had to establish not only the genuineness of need, but to what unit of government belonged the duty of meeting it. We are all-too familiar with the limited scope of that word *belong* in much of relief practice. The person's *need* belongs to this town or city, this county or state, but perhaps in no other discernible way is he recognized as belonging as a person, with the status accorded to the most favored citizens. All too often relief applicants have received no more acceptance than a grudging care for their minimum needs. They have been abused in the newspapers, as public charges if not as "chiselers" and "ne'er do wells," they have been put to work at starvation wages, treated like outcasts, in some places even denied the ballot.

What are the consequences to a community when it reduces any group of its citizens to a declassed minority?* Long and bitter experience, from the time of

---

* In point of numbers those on relief were actually a majority in some communities during the depression, but in power and influence were kept in the status of a minority.

the Elizabethan Poor Laws on, has shown a resulting deterioration of human qualities, a pauperism in which children grew up to repeat the same conditions for the rearing of their children, a bitter resentment against "charity" which often increased the habit of demanding, in proportion, as hope of rehabilitation receded. Relief which is too niggardly ever to restore to self-support increases the relief burden on the community a thousandfold. That the whole community must take the responsibility when its members are unable to command an opportunity to work to meet their necessities is apparent, not only on moral grounds but in economic fact. No power but the right to tax can raise funds sufficient to the needs created in an economic depression. The spending of those funds is spending for the survival of the community itself.

How does this philosophy of public assistance gain acceptance in our national life? A few in every community, at the top in terms of income and power over the labor of others, would deny altogether the philosophy just expressed. They would say that a community owes its citizens nothing. This does not apply to such benefits as government subsidies to business, or legislation favorable to profits. It applies only, in the minds of this comfortable minority, to relief of need. They would consider it good public policy that starvation should force men to work at any wage which may be offered. From this orientation, there must always be an excess of unemployed labor from which to choose. Relief, if it exists, must be kept low enough so that no one will be tempted to refuse any kind of job, and must be surrounded with the most onerous conditions. Although, as we have said, a relatively small proportion of the total population is impelled by its economic position to resent the interference of public assistance with its labor supply, a much larger number of people, in small businesses and the professions, and even among wage workers themselves, are influenced to think in much the same way by the opinion-forming media of press and radio, through appeal to their fear of increasing tax burdens.

It is impossible to conceive that social work worthy of being called in any sense professional can be practised under such a philosophy. Throughout the history of public assistance, there has been a healthy struggle against the degradation of human beings by the very means designed to keep them barely in existence. The thousands of people who were drawn in to the administration of public assistance programs in the United States in the 1930's, poorly selected and unprepared as they often were for the great responsibilities they had to carry, were learning by experience what need meant and how to meet it. The real challenge to their skill was not in the task of assembling facts to prove need and residence, but in ability to keep relief recipients in the stream of community living, and in full use of their citizenship. This paid off to the community in the matter of helping people to use resources they still had, in themselves, or latent in their situation. It paid off still more in good citizenship in place of pauperism and crime. This is the unanswerable argument for the use of the best skills of professional social casework in the administration of public assistance. It is individualization of service, and keeping people aware of their true status as citizens in a democracy which makes the difference between deterioration of human beings and their actual growth under adversity.

Social workers in public assistance have always been placed by their communities under severe handicaps, with little community understanding of their work and never enough money to make possible a decent standard of living for relief recipients. This would have been even more apparent had it not been true that many employed workers were also not able to earn enough to give their families a decent standard. Public assistance workers have been forced to work under laws and administrative rulings which, in many cases, were destructive because of their denial to clients of initiative and responsibility. One example is giving relief in kind when clients would actually save money by shopping for themselves with a cash grant. Some of the worst abuses have been mitigated by protests organized in the community by groups of clients and by other citizens who cared what happened to people in need. Some improvements have come about through the organization of social workers in labor unions, so that they could be better protected, not only in their own conditions of work, but in their efforts to arouse the community to take more responsibility for its public services.

All of this experience in public assistance (in which the conflict is still acute between responsibility for sound public service and the use of needy people as a depressed source of surplus labor power) is a vivid demonstration that the key question is that of *responsibility*. If need is in one part of the population, and the responsibility for meeting it is in quite another part, the result is deterioration of the needy people who are left without responsibility. Inevitably, also, the result is that taking charge of the fate of a declassed group presents an opportunity to exploit them in one way or another. If the responsibility for meeting need resides in the whole body of citizens, in which needy people themselves belong, then theirs is the responsibility, equally with all other citizens, for *their* relief administration. They need not passively submit to subhuman treatment. They need not, feeling that they are victims, ask better treatment with apologies. They must, as citizens, demand better public assistance. Without acceptance of a decent standard of living for those who must depend on relief, labor has no floor below which wages may not fall. The whole community must demand more adequate grants to those who are unable to earn a living, because the entire business community suffers in a time of depression from lack of purchasing power, and keeping up basic income stimulates business. The public must demand adequate relief because, without it health suffers and illness spreads, not only from home to home but to the mortgaging of the precious lives of the next generation. Plain economic common sense demands diffusion of responsibility throughout the whole community.

Social workers in public assistance, then, have an immensely important service to perform when they build up and maintain the full sense of citizenship in the people with whom they work. The American people have shown a growing appreciation of the responsibility of government for insuring to all its citizens the opportunity for a healthy and socially useful life, but this entails the responsibility of all citizens in a democracy for their government. It may well be that in the future the discharge of this responsibility will take the form of much more comprehensive social insurance for all hazards, including that of involuntary unemployment. The least we can do, after economic breakdown has deprived a family of its means of earning a living, is to make public assistance a *right*, in which a citizen can, and must, exercise his responsibility, as one who *belongs* in the fullest sense.

3. Comparing Concepts of Eligibility

The concept of eligibility began to be used in private social agencies when public assistance investigations for proof of need made it seem that private agencies also should have a more professional, less haphazard, basis for selection of clients. It was not at first realized how different was the meaning of the term in public and private social work. Private agencies see their clients as *outside* until they are invited *in*, and there is no basis for thinking of them as belonging (as in public welfare) by virtue of being residents in the community. Private agencies, if they are freed by a good public assistance program from responsibility for subsistence relief, no longer have in their hands to offer the necessities which mean life or death, along with which people are forced to take other benefits whether they want them or not. Practically everything that a private agency can offer in these days—counseling, opportunities of education or recreation, some forms of medical care—are meaningless unless the person wants them. There is validity, then, if demand for services outruns resources, in taking applications with some appraisal of ability to make use of what is offered, as well as the strength of desire for it. The tests are, as we have seen, very difficult to devise or apply. In addition, the appeals to the community, by which funds are raised for the support of private agencies, create, more and more, the feeling that private agencies belong to the community, and are not the possession of the small group which shapes their policies. People who want the service of these agencies wish to know why they are not eligible if others are, especially if they have contributed to the Community Fund. Private agencies cannot afford to be arbitrary or obscure about their selection of clients, any more than can the public services. If they are the advance scouts, working on the frontiers of human need which the public services may later come to occupy, there is especial point in their being most responsive to what people want when they really have some choice.

We shall study in the next chapter an example of a private social agency which was able to work in co-operation with a membership organization, a trade union, to meet emergency needs of merchant seamen in time of war. Here, eligibility was determined by the fact of being an active seaman, and, in that particular agency, a member of the union. The only selection at intake was in choice of services, what the seaman wanted out of what could be offered. It was an extra-ordinary opportunity for the social workers engaged in the project to see how a group employed in one industry would respond to a social agency which was not public, but which they could think of as their own.

IV. Members Entitled to What?

1. In a Membership Organization

The National Maritime Union was a young, rapidly growing organization in the terrible spring of 1943. It was one of a number of maritime unions affiliated with the Congress of Industrial Organizations, and had contracts with more than half of the shipping companies in the Merchant Marine. It brought together in its membership among unlicensed seamen (i.e., exclusive of ship's officers) three distinct occupations: deckworkers, from ordinary seamen up to bosuns carrying supervisory responsibility; engine room workers, from wipers to junior engineers; and food workers, from messmen to cooks and stewards. It had won improvements in wages which made it possible for the first time for a seaman to support a family.

Early in 1943, more than five thousand of the Union's members had laid down their lives to keep the ships sailing, when convoys of ships setting out across the dark ocean were attacked and sunk both from the air and from underseas. Seamen who had survived torpedo attacks as many as five times grimly kept sailing for their dead brothers, and gave themselves no rest. So many of the old-timers, the experienced seamen, were gone, and the boys coming into the industry from Selective Service Class IIB were so unused even to smooth sailing that the Union had a tremendous job of education to do. The Union opened a school for training ordinary seamen (beginners) to take examinations for the rank of able-bodied seaman (skilled mariner). This school was approved and taken over by the government when the need for personnel to man the ships became an acute war problem.

The National Maritime Union was at that time under the able leadership of men who had been tested in the labor upsurge of 1937. It had elected officers under a democratic constitution, and had set up its own hiring hall, with impartial rotation of jobs to men holding the proper government endorsements of their skill. This system replaced the hiring which had been done by shipping companies from graft-ridden agencies in waterfront saloons and boarding houses. Most of the elected officers of the Union carried their heavy responsibilities with great courage and devotion to the interests of the members.

At the 1941 Convention of the Union, it had been voted to establish a personal service department, to take care of personal problems of the members which were an increasing burden on the elected officers. An old seaman, equipped with a desk and a secretary, took charge of the new service. There were urgent questions of claims for injuries and personal losses suffered at sea. War brought a multitude of problems, from small services needed (like procuring ration books when seamen had not been ashore to register for them, and arrangements for buying more than one pair of shoes when a long voyage was in prospect), up to help to distressed families in locating seamen who were often stranded by injuries in parts of the world from which it was not easy to get return passage. As casualty lists lengthened, there was need for help to bereaved families with immediate living problems, and in filing claims for War Risk Insurance. The secretary, a young woman who had been a portrait painter and had turned to labor organization to express her love for people in a more significant way, was learning how to use the structure of social agencies in the community for services to seamen and families.

In the early months of the war, the Union had urged that the government, through the War Shipping Administration (since the shipping companies were then operating under government subsidies and control) should do something to remedy the neglect of the needs of merchant seamen which had been a national disgrace for many years. Seamen, who in the first war year had suffered more casualties in ship sinkings than had the armed forces, were excluded from the facilities of the Red Cross and United Service Organizations. They could not find decent housing or recreation in the ports crowded with war personnel. They were often stranded away from home, sick or severely injured, and consumed with worry about their families with whom they could not communicate. Their families were often left without support until red tape in some distant part of the world could be unwound. With all this, there was a critical need for seamen to man the ships, which were daily coming from the shipyards, to carry supplies to the armed forces overseas.

United Seamen's Service was organized in the fall of 1942, with a Board consisting of representatives of government (the War Shipping Administration), shipping companies, maritime unions and the general public. It was financed by the War Fund. Its residence hotels and recreation clubs in active ports around the world made a spot of home for seamen, and its personal service workers helped to reduce a thousand worries for them and their families. On the principle that it would place its facilities anywhere that seamen were assembled in large numbers, it sent recreation workers to the Union Hall of the NMU early in 1943. Thousands of seamen were there waiting for jobs to be called out on the loud-speakers and posted on the bulletins. On the same principle, the USS offered a personal service worker and a loan fund for seamen's emergencies to the personal service department of the Union. The writer became the United Seamen's Service representative at the National Maritime Union Hall in New York, and was with the joint project until it closed in December, 1947.

Professional social workers were immediately curious to know how a professional service would function in the setting of a labor union. By the spring of 1943, the NMU had already begun to use professional workers in other ways. Out of the same respect for knowledge and skill which had led it to establish its own upgrading school for seamanship, the Union had engaged an educational director with experience in university teaching, and had another university teacher giving courses along with experienced seamen in its school. It had professional journalists on its newspaper staff, and had engaged a social worker with a master's degree for its now reorganized personal service department. Professional social workers coming in to this setting (and there was soon to be a staff of seven) would find an unhampered opportunity to use their skills, and at the same time a challenge (which is of the essence of professional skill) to adapt to the way of life, the culture and mores, of this particular sector of a great industry.

Briefly, the mechanics of cooperation between the USS, a private war service agency, and the NMU, a labor union, were as follows: The Union furnished the professional director and assistant director (the secretary of the old personal service office), and a clerical staff for the newly reorganized personal service, plus office equipment and quarters convenient to the shipping hall in the national headquarters building. A host of minor services, such as information, selective service and rationing problems, and taking care of a mass of inquiries by correspondence, was the responsibility of the clerical (or, better, technical) staff, under the supervision of the professionally trained director of the department. The USS furnished professionally qualified caseworkers who were also acceptable to the Union as members of the Social Service Employees Union. The USS made available a fund for loans to seamen, which were urgently necessary in an extremely hazardous industry in which there were often long waits for adjudication of claims, and in which emergencies were of daily occurrence.

Under the terms of cooperation, the USS representative was administratively responsible to the director of the personal service department in all matters of union policy, and contacts with the union officials, thus having channeled to her all the resources within the Union. Similarly, the Union director of Personal Service was responsible to the USS representative for carrying out USS policy in regard to loans, and could use, through her, all the resources of USS. The USS representative acted as case supervisor of the staff of social caseworkers. The department cooperated closely with the social services of the Marine Hospitals, and the Merchant Marine Rest Centers where seamen could steady their nerves and gain strength to ship out again after weeks of grueling work in the convoys of ships sailing under daily and nightly threat of attack by bombs or torpedoes. The social agencies in the community were used whenever their services were available to seamen or their families.

The group of social caseworkers who went in to this cooperative undertaking as a war service were enthusiastic about the opportunity to extend the frontier of social work into a great industry. They saw this as a very different venture from that of counseling in industry as it is sponsored by management. Here the workers who used the service would be the sponsors, because of its location in their own union hall. These social workers were conscious of the gains in living standards which seamen had made since they had formed the Union in 1937, and were aware of the advantage of a strong, democratic labor union over a social agency, when it came to improvements in the welfare of thousands of workers and their families. These professional workers felt that now something new had been added to what a union can achieve without personal attention to individual members, and they were proud to bring that new personal touch. They learned only gradually how much that was new, or not sufficiently understood, was to be added to their theory and practice of social work, by this opportunity to be "closer to people."

2. Selection Among Services

A membership organization which sets up any kind of service for individuals has an intake problem quite different from that of a social agency which determines eligibility for its benefits. In a membership organization, it is not a question of selecting, from those who are outside, the people who meet the conditions for admission. All the members, and these may run into thousands in an organization which is large enough to consider a welfare department, are equally entitled to the benefits of their membership. If conditions are set up, they must apply to all alike, and must be explainable in terms that all can understand. Discrimination among applicants on the basis of a study of their needs can be explained, but such an explanation must show how two situations are really different, and that one individual is not favored over another on personal grounds. When there is dissatisfaction with a decision, a democratic trade union has procedure for appeal to elected officials whose function it is to guard the interests of the members, and whose decision, in turn, can be challenged in membership meeting, or in the pages of the union newspaper.

If this membership control seems shocking to some social workers who believe that they are responsible to nobody but their own conscience before God, it is useful to be reminded, as were the personal service workers at the NMU Hall, that in a social agency there is interposed between the caseworker and God a Board of Directors whose interests are more remote from those

of the clients than are the interests of officials elected
by their fellow members. If it is objected that union
members know nothing of professional practice, we find
a similar lack in many board members of social agencies. Responsibility to one's clientele is a healthy corrective of practice which no agency can afford to be
without. The group of caseworkers at NMU found it
stimulating, for instance, to receive a referral like the
following from a union representative whose duty it
was to take up with the U.S. Coast Guard cases of al-
leged breach of discipline, or violations of safety regulations:

> "Please see that Brother Lee gets a good medi-
> cal examination. He opened an oil valve in the en-
> gine room, and said he couldn't shut it. He might
> have caused a serious accident. If he can't do his
> work he should be off the ships, but maybe there
> is something wrong with him."

It was found that there was—a disease of the central
nervous system. Personal Service of the Union, and the
medical social service department of the Merchant Marine Medical Center entered into intensive cooperation
to solve this man's problem. It was a healthy professional exercise for social workers to give back to the
source of referral an interpretation looking toward helping a whole group of men to be alert to signs of medical disability.

Responsibility of a caseworker to an organized
group which is at once her board of directors and her
clientele is, in part, a responsibility for knowing what
the members want in the way of help. Being close to
their daily lives, in an association with their own or-

ganization so that they feel free to say what they think, is an immense advantage. What *did* they think?

The requests that came to the personal service department were predominantly for loans, outside of minor services which connected the seaman or his family with needed information. Both groups of services reflected the dislocations of wartime shipping, and the marginal economic status of seamen's families. Men might not be paid until legal questions involved in a ship-sinking were settled. Injured men had to wait for compensation until medical prognoses could be made. In spite of the much-advertised prosperity of seamen who received war bonuses, many had simply used bonus money to pay debts dating from the depression, or to buy much-needed furniture or make a down payment on a home. Few families had savings to cover any extra expense occasioned by illness or a death in the family.

In contrast, then, to the usual private social agency, the resources of the personal service department were largely employed with economic problems. Around these were clustered all sorts of other problems, including those of emotions and of social relationships which most agencies consider the major focus of their work. The seamen were appreciative of an opportunity to talk about these, and to have what help could be given in the brief time they were ashore. What was apparent, however, was that economic problems were a major and constant source of anxiety to this group of employed workers.

Many times neither the seaman nor the personal service department had a solution for very real and urgent needs. Conditions in this extra-hazardous industry had, over a long period, created situations for which there was no immediate remedy. Imperfect as was the adjustment between Personal Service and the needs it tried to meet, one characteristic was always present—its welcome to all comers.

3. A Welcome for All

How *can* one welcome everybody when human strength and time are definitely limited, and when demands which are always enough to occupy a staff full time are periodically excessive? Personal Service found no satisfactory solution, but clarified essential elements of the problem of disparity between human needs and the means of meeting them.

1. The attitude of welcome must be there for everyone. Waiting one's turn could be understood, even though it tried the patience, because all assignments for jobs on ships were also made in turn. Waiting must have its reward, however. Each man in the crowd in the waiting room must be assured that he would not be forgotten, or his request slighted. The caseworker at the application desk needed a light touch, a bit of humor, to ease the tension of so many in trouble. She must not become so absorbed in seeing individuals one by one as to sense the whole group only as a source of irritation to her.

2. The sifting, as applicants stated their requests in turn, must deal quickly and efficiently with such minor services as giving information, or direction to other kinds of service in the building. A clerical assistant working with the case-

worker was invaluable in taking care of telephone calls and "handling traffic." The sifting process itself, however, called for the skills of the most experienced caseworkers on the staff. It was found that no technical method could catch problems requiring instant appraisal of many complex factors. For instance, when the intake sifting was in the hands of a very sensitive clerical worker, a man was one day turned away on a valid technicality. A caseworker happened to see him, and to note some peculiarities in his appearance, particularly signs of serious physical maladjustment. A few questions brought out that he was just back from four years in a prison camp in the Pacific, that he was sick and penniless, because of some slip in the usual arrangements for care of such cases, and was so discouraged that this rebuff, in his eyes, was just conclusive evidence that nobody cared what happened to him. After it was arranged that a caseworker should always be present at the intake desk, the minor and the serious problems could be better allocated. For the latter, an appointment with a caseworker in the privacy of her office was made for the same day, if possible. The caseworkers served in turn at the intake desk, to keep their sensitivity alert in both kinds of interviewing.

3. The talk with the caseworker in her office might be brief, but it must allow time for a man to tell his story in his own way. The sense that each applicant had of belonging (without having to face acceptance or rejection at the door) eliminated much of the resistance which social agencies ex-

pect to find, and talk was usually spontaneous, saving hours of time in establishing rapport. When the caseworker asked questions, it was to reach as quickly as possible an understanding of the problems that could be dealt with immediately, before the man sailed, and those that might be worked through, perhaps with his family, during his absence. Every solution was talked over in terms of his active participation.

4. When loans had to be refused, or other requests could not be met, how could a welcoming attitude be conveyed to the applicant? The caseworkers found many, as in other social agencies, who came with the hope of getting rid of a troublesome problem, and who could not understand a refusal except as rejection of themselves. Many had met so much deprivation, race discrimination, and even persecution, that these reactions were understandable. The caseworkers learned, however, that they invited misunderstandings if they said no, without first saying, in some fashion, "We want to help you. Let's talk it over, and if there is nothing we can do we will tell you so frankly." Preoccupation of the caseworker with the decision, to give or not to give, rather than with seeing the person and his need, was sure to cut off the opportunity to help the man with his adjustment to the refusal.

The casework tradition that it is important to sift out as quickly as possible those who are not eligible to receive what they ask, was not applicable in the union setting. Here, nobody was *out*, and a person who could not be given a loan might be helped in some other way. To concentrate on saying no was to miss important clues to a real service which could be given. Trade union members, moreover, have a rather realistic acceptance of genuine lack of resources. Their activities as a union group tend to overcome childish attitudes of asking for everything, from daily bread to jam, from a powerful parent-person. They mature in learning that what they get they must work for (even if that means standing together and fighting for it in collective bargaining), and they are more ready than social workers to seek group solutions where these are possible. The following is a case in point:

> Early in the life of the personal service department, seamen began coming for loans if they found, after assignment to a ship, that there were no living quarters ready for them. Typically, the man would have paid bills, sent money to his family in another state, perhaps, saving just enough for himself until he could get another job assignment. On reaching the ship, he found that the galley stove was being repaired, and no cooking could be done for several days. Carpenters were working in the crew's quarters, and there were no bunks. It was Friday and Captain and Purser were off till Monday, while a skeleton crew stood watch on the ship. The office of the shipping company refused to pay the allowance for room and meals due the crew until quarters were available, until five days of work time had been completed.

This was a real emergency to a man in a strange city without a cent in his pocket, and loans for the week-end were made at first by the personal service department. This policy was soon reconsidered in consultation with Union officials. It was evident that if one man knew about Personal Service there were others in the same plight who did not, and a preventive solution should be found. The Union arranged to have official reports include whether a ship was "sleeping and feeding," in the description of the jobs called out in the shipping hall. It was then the responsibility of the man who had no money for subsistence for a few days to take a job only on a ship which was ready for the crew. The Union also did what it could to see that shipping companies made businesslike arrangements for paying subsistence allowances promptly, and encouraged members to take initiative in insisting on their rights under the Union contract. Social agencies sometimes prolong bad conditions by subsidizing them when they ought to be removed. It is not often the case, however, that an agency is in a position to know as quickly as did Personal Service, just what it is doing, and to be as close to the possibility of corrective action.

To draw together our discussion of what the intake problem is in a social service in a large membership organization, the basic fact is that admission is inclusive, not exclusive, and sifting is directed to sorting requests according to the service needed, and what can be given, rather than to eliminating applicants. Each person is entitled to the fundamental service of a diagnosis by a professional person of what his need is and where it can be met. If a referral elsewhere is indicated, the casework skills needed to prepare the applicant and the other agency are also offered.

There is another aspect of being a social agency which belongs to its clientele. Not only do applicants belong in the agency when they first come, without having to be selected for its benefits, but the relationship is a continuing one. Suppose a referral to a family agency is worked out with care to see that the basis is laid for a good relationship there. Suppose, however, that the applicant is disturbed about some of the procedures, feels a little strange, and does not like to ask questions. He comes in again to his Union department to talk it over. There is no formal insistence that, since he has gone elsewhere, he must take up his difficulty there. He is always welcome in his Union, and the misunderstandings are worked out, sometimes in a telephone conversation in which the man listens and takes part. If social agencies wonder about this, being used to taking title to clients as in the conveyance of real estate, there is no answer except that a man is never cut off from his union, any more than from his family, and that improvement of his use of other agencies is always a part of the function of his personal service department.

Among the leaders of the NMU who had been responsible for setting up a personal service department, it was an accepted principle that a union should not duplicate social services available elsewhere. It was best for the membership to support community services, particularly public services open to all citizens, and to strengthen thereby their own ties with the community while they helped to improve services for everyone. It was desirable to have their own personal service only because the members needed, for a period at least, an agency to make known to them how they could use community services, and a place where problems peculiar to an especially hazardous industry would be immediately understood. Cooperation with United Seamen's Service, a private community agency geared to an understanding of seamen, was an excellent way of becoming a more active part of the community.

With this background of experience in a social service department which was financed partly by a private war agency and partly by a labor union, we have an opportunity to explore the concept of eligibility for service as it applies in the setting of a membership organization. As we review some case examples, we shall find that, as to acceptance of the person, membership in the union entitled him to whatever the department could offer. The policy of United Seamen's Service did not limit this right, since it was also inclusive. Its service was open to all active seamen (as well as to those not members of this Union in other centers). What could be offered in the way of financial assistance varied with the availability of funds, and with certain USS policies in regard to the kinds of need for which they could be used. The right to be served was always present.

4.   One Who Hardly Felt He Belonged

The first example is that of a young man whose major problem was that he felt he did not *belong*, anywhere. If he had not been a member of the Union, and hence did belong in a sense, it is certain the personal service department would never have heard of him. His need was definite and concrete—for food and a place to sleep until he could get a job.

Philip Keene, a young man of twenty-two, had come in and gone out of the department several times before he gathered courage to ask for a loan. He was an oiler (a skilled rating in the engine room), but could not get a job immediately because he had come from another port, and had registered for a job when there were too many oilers ahead of him. He was very tense, nervous and thin. He was ashamed to borrow because he had spent his money foolishly on this shore leave. He had seen a lot of enemy action, having gone through the battle of Sicily, and had been three times on ships which were torpedoed. On one of these ship sinkings, he had spent a week in a life boat on the Atlantic, and half the men in the boat had died before they were rescued. He insisted that he was all right, except for "this," a marked tremor in his right arm. Later, he let slip the remark that he had a bad heart. He blamed himself for drinking too much. He "went to sea too early," at age fourteen, sailing with his father who was a captain, now retired.

It took several interviews, in which loans were arranged for a day or two at a time, before he was relaxed enough to tell more about his family who were living in Canada. He was the youngest of fourteen, all better educated than he. He said he was a "black sheep," though he added, "They all love me best." Whether this was true, or only fantasy, he did not go home oftener than once in several years. He felt caught in an endless round of sea trips, broken only by short leaves in which he spent his money in wild sprees and shipped again.

It was easy to suspect a war neurosis, perhaps over-laying deeper maladjustments, but Philip would by no means be persuaded to stay ashore for treatment with a psychiatrist at a rest center. He prided himself on staying away from hospitals. The caseworker saw her job, aside from making it possible by small loans for him to sleep in a bed instead of in the subways, and to have decent food instead of handouts in waterfront saloons, to help him to relax enough so that he would be open to persuasion to go to the Medical Center for a check-up. She suspected that he had a good deal of fear of what the doctors might find. She did not succeed in getting him to a clinic before he sailed, and could only hope that routine shipping examinations might at some time bring out what his health needs were. Al-though she failed in this objective, the caseworker did gain some clues to his personality that definitely af-fected her way of handling the loans, and her way of drawing him out on his visits to the office.

Here was a boy who was separated from normal family and community life at age fourteen, but was, so he said, kept under strict discipline by his father on the ship. If he had been a spoiled or delinquent boy before that, as one suspects because he was taken out of school so early, such a method of treatment could do nothing else than shut off social contacts and inde-pendent decisions which would have made it possible for him to mature emotionally in a normal way. His contacts with women had been on the waterfronts of ports all over the world. He had never had social oppor-tunities elsewhere, and was convinced that decent peo-ple ashore would never associate with him. During the interviews, lasting about three weeks, the caseworker tried to give him a different point of view about himself, to overcome his hopelessness about ever amounting to anything, and in some simple ways to build up his resources for a different way of spending his shore leaves. She introduced him to the Union's credit union bank, to which he could alot some of his pay monthly, to have it in a safer place than his pocket when he came off a ship. He could buy good clothes, go to a canteen and see a different kind of girls, have a good time of a different kind. He tried a canteen and liked it, and even met a girl he could talk to. Such a reorientation might not make an appreciable difference in a neurosis which may have been of longer duration than his war service, but no other form of treatment was available to him on terms which his fears would allow him to take. This social treatment did make a slight break in a vicious cycle of inferiority feeling, low companions, fears for his health, a conviction that he would die young and was not worth saving anyway. The caseworker gave him some hope of being like other young men, eventually having a home and family of his own such as he began to realize he wanted. She gave him a simple device for saving to buy what he might want most, some respect for himself, some slight degree of social experience. This might, or might not, make a difference in his anticipation and planning for his next leave. At least this brief treatment opened the door to new incentives and a more normal outlook.

5. One Who Didn't Conform

The following case raises more serious questions, by current standards of determining eligibility for casework service from private social agencies. Would it be worth the time of most agencies to give this kind of service to a person who did not know how to formulate his problem, who disliked social workers and was not appreciative, who did not even cooperate very well? In a membership organization he was eligible because he belonged.

Union brother John Dere was sixty-one when he first came to Personal Service at NMU Hall, but he looked much older, thin and yellow and tired. He had become used to thinking of himself as old, and to feeling that people put things over on him because he was old. He said once that he spent his money because he wouldn't live long anyway.

He used Personal Service during the war as a place to make loans when he was "broke," loans which he scrupulously repaid. Once he lost his wallet. Another time, after long hours at the wheel on a Lakes steamer, an old injury to his foot bothered him again, and he could not ship for a week or two. Again, it was a cold which laid him up. He refused Rest Center care, for he said he must be earning, yet he looked too frail and shaky to keep working. He had no relatives, and, as a seaman, no old age security.

It seemed to the personal service worker that Brother Dere would inevitably have to take a rest after each trip, and would probably have to lose considerable time because of illness. He was too worn out to fill a place in an industry requiring much exertion, yet because he had no other way of living he needed to keep working as long as he could, perhaps in a protected job such as that of fire-watchman on a ship.

Brother Dere's financial and health problems were complicated by what his hardships and his fears had done to his personality. He hated hospitals, and had a long history which gave substance to his attitude. Like most seamen, he had often gone without medical care aboard ship, and had been impatient of delays in treatment in crowded clinics ashore. He was irritated at what seemed to him senseless procedures, and was both unwilling to claim his just rights and too stubbornly independent to cooperate when someone tried to help him.

With a background of three years of contacts with Personal Service on very temporary practical problems, Brother Dere came again in 1947 to fill out an application for Unemployment Insurance benefits, newly opened to seamen by Federal legislation. The personal service worker at the intake desk saw more than a confused old man who needed help with a complicated technical procedure. She saw a man who was obviously depressed, and probably facing a pretty hopeless future. She arranged for an interviewer to see him, and "pull the situation together." While the intake worker explained to him what shipping discharges he would need to bring tomorrow, she tried to draw him out, casually but sympathetically, about his outlook for retirement from seafaring. He had no plans to report, and wanted no sympathy, so she got little except his dislike of a well-endowed Seamen's Home. Next day, a large part of the interview in the caseworker's office was spent in helping him to recall dates and names of shipping companies, and telling him where he could get information which was missing because some of his documents were lost. Some verification was started by telephone.

When the caseworker told him that it would be at least two weeks before his eligibility for benefits could be established by the State Unemployment Insurance Division, he was disturbed and angry. "What am I going to do tonight?" The personal service department had at this time no money for loans. There followed a talk about his need of help, his right to it, that the city Department of Public Welfare was not a "charity" like the religious missions he knew, and how an application could be made. It was explained in detail how he would have some questions to answer, how his needs would be budgeted, how a check would be sent to him. Reluctantly, since he had no other choice, Brother Dere agreed to apply. He heard the caseworker speak on the telephone with the intake supervisor at the Department of Welfare about him, and was given a letter of referral, so that he would have something to take with him. He knew that the emergency nature of his need was emphasized, and that temporary aid could be given the same day.

The next day Brother Dere was back, after a telephone call had come from the Welfare Department interviewer to the effect that he had said he could "manage" until the investigation was completed. His rueful account was that when they said, "Can you manage until we get to your application?" he thought they would not help him anyway for a while, so he said yes. He supposed he could "bum a nickel for a cup of coffee," and had spent the night walking around the streets. When this was discussed by telephone between the two agencies, the Welfare worker indicated that it was the man's problem and responsibility to state whether he could manage or not. The Department of Welfare did arrange to give a temporary emergency check, and a monthly budget check would follow if it was needed.

There followed complications for several days, in which Brother Dere was very hungry, angry and discouraged, could not get to see the person to whom he was directed, thought everyone was "passing the buck." Even the U.S. mail seemed to fail him by delaying his identification card so that when he got his check he could not cash it. Then there were complications in his getting his Unemployment Insurance. He had, in fact, been afraid to apply because he thought he would "get in trouble" if he was receiving relief. Then, when he was persuaded to do something about badly needed glasses and dentures, he could hardly control his disgust at the Marine Hospital enough to go through the process of being examined. When he was offered carfare home from the clinic by a hospital social worker, and she gave him a voucher for it, he "blew up." "She should have trusted me," he complained. He walked the four miles to his room rather than take it. When the personal service worker at the Union compared the hospital vouchers to those used here to get money from the cashier, he said, "Oh, here, that's entirely different." He refused the first dental appointment, a month away, because they had no business to make him wait so long. The personal service worker drew him out about his experiences with hospitals in many ports, over many years, and accepted his attitudes as quite natural. When he felt understood, Brother Dere could see for himself that his attitudes got in his way.

Brother Dere then dropped it all, and went to sea for a month. It was still another month later that he came to Personal Service again, his pay used up and his Unemployment Insurance application in a snarl. He had been sleeping in parks for a week. He could not apply for Department of Welfare Home Relief unless he had a residence. He absolutely refused the City Shelter where, he believed, "only bums" went. To his mind, he had lost both his relief and unemployment insurance because he had worked, although it was "such a little, temporary job." He felt old and shunted about.

This time, Personal Service was able to help him with a little money for food until his Unemployment Insurance application could be checked, and enough for a room overnight, so that he could get his application to the Welfare Department started from that address. This time, he went through with the application, and began to trust the Welfare Department enough to see how he could use it at times when he would "get stuck" and could not get a job. The personal service worker was fulfilling the function of connecting this man of many personal problems with social resources which were available to him, but which he could not use without help. It took much time and patience to bring him through to the achievement of establishing his own relationship with the Department of Welfare, so that he could go to it at times when his earning power failed.

If benefit to society is a criterion of a valid function of a social agency, what had this old, sick man to contribute the more, after time was spent to get him to receive public assistance? Does it benefit the community to have casework service given to its relatively unproductive members?

This question recalls an old dilemma of social work. If agencies select the most helpless cases, they invite the criticism that they coddle the weak at the expense of the most productive members of society. They give grounds for the "stigma" which has traditionally been placed upon the clients of social agencies. If, on the other hand, agencies select those who are capable, and are in situations from which they can extricate themselves with not too great an expenditure of social service time and money, it may be argued that these are people who might make their way without help, and would profit from being left to do so. Private agencies have seen an opportunity to avoid this dilemma by depositing the most needy and least productive cases (as they estimated them) on the doorstep of the public agency, keeping clear of the stigma attached to supposedly inferior people by selecting clients who would be able to cooperate well with private agency ways of working. This does not avoid, however, a conflict over determining the value of a person to society. The only groups in history which seem to be completely logical and without conflict about this are the supermen of fascist regimes. They decide what racial stocks are to be marked for extermination, and wipe them out by mass murder with full confidence in their formula for fitness to survive. A tragic lesson for our profession is to be learned from the fate of German social workers who were employed by the Nazis to assist in carrying out their decrees, or were replaced by party members who would do so, and would act as informers and propaganda agents.* Social workers who have the spirit and standard of a profession can never be as clear as this as to who are and who are not worthwhile.

From the point of view which we are taking in these explorations, there is an element of begging-the-question in the assumption that casework service is either a solution for unproductive members of society, or that refusing to invest in casework for them leaves society better off by the amount of money saved. Unproductive members of society are symptoms of serious social ills that cannot long be ignored. Incidentally, some unproductive members of society contribute to social agencies, rather than coming to them as clients. In the client group, however, John Dere may be taken as an example:

> He need not have been crippled in health and warped in personality at age sixty-one. Most of his life he had worked hard for a pittance that was too small to permit marriage and the rearing of children who might have helped him in his old age. He had slept in airless fo'castles, eaten bad food, been exposed to tropical diseases, gone untreated when he was sick or injured. Somebody profited by the difference between what he produced in keeping merchant ships moving, and what he was paid. Society paid the cost of taking care of him, meagerly and periodically, in his cheerless old age. A social agency which happened to be located in his Union (or he would never have found it) did the skillful and patient work

* Friedlander, Walter A., "Social Work Under the Nazi Regime," *Social Work Today*, Vol. VII, November 1939.

necessary to connect him with public assistance and insurance benefits to which he was entitled, but which he could not reach without help. This social service solved nothing in the conditions which produced this kind of old age, but it made one human being feel less neglected and more able to keep on working part-time for a few more years. Having Personal Service there undoubtedly heightened morale for others in the working span of life who feared being utterly cast aside when they too should become disabled. John Dere had already contributed to society, at heavy cost to himself, and merited what he needed. An intelligent solution, however, would have to go back to the conditions which produced a John Dere, and which had denied him a sense of belonging to the whole of society, as well as to the smaller group of his union.

v. Don't You
Spoil People?

1. Why Social Workers Fear Doing Too Much

For fifty years social workers have been trying to live down the allegation that for this work "All you need is a kind heart." Becoming professional has meant trying to prove that one has a head, and trying to find some way to use it to advantage in the affairs of other people. Only comparatively recently has the term, *warm*, been safely included in references for social workers. Professional literature has made it clear, however, that being a *warm* person did not mean identifying the client with one's self. One must maintain some "professional" aloofness in order to help him. Although it is pleasant to do kind things for people, is that really casework? Or is it satisfying some personal need of the caseworker?

There is no doubt that the trend in social work, as it has become more professional, has been away from kindness as such to activities that accomplish something that the agency regards as its function. There are those who think that the personal service department of the National Maritime Union deserted the standards of professional social casework to go back to sentimental errand-running such as was characteristic of the pre-professional history of social work. They would say that if working for a membership organization means that one has to do what the members want done, then it isn't professional social work. Suppose we analyze these concepts for a moment; the social worker's personal need to be kind, and the idea that it weakens clients to have things done for them:

The history of the psychiatric trend in social casework shows that the spotlight of personal analysis was turned first on the clients, particularly those who were mentally disturbed or in trouble with the law, then upon the motives of good people, artists, writers, and doers-of-good in general to see why they were that way, and, finally, upon social workers themselves. Why did they choose to be social workers, and how were they using their personal desires in their work? Their own histories were often illuminating, as they had to produce them as exercises in schools of social work, or as they re-lived them in being psychoanalyzed. Social workers were found to be, often, people who had suffered a deprived childhood, who could not solve their own problems as easily as they could try to solve those of others. They often longed to make others more comfortable than they had been. Discomfort in childhood had not always been physical, but many discovered when they studied psychiatry that their handicaps went back to rejecting parents, and to rivalries with more favored brothers and sisters. Training in social work became a process of learning to be "objective" about these personal hurts, so as not to have to thwart parent-persons among their clients, or favor the underdog who reminded them unconsciously of themselves. Some caseworkers were labeled "masochistic," the martyr type, laboring ceaselessly to do good to others and allowing themselves almost no pleasure except through others. Psychiatry described them as able to live only if they could turn their natural aggression back upon themselves, and find release in the self-martyrdom of ceaseless service to others.

The period in the growth of social work into a profession when it concentrated much attention upon psychiatry brought out real dangers and pointed the way to real goals in training social workers to use their personalities professionally. In a sound course of training, a professional self can be developed which will enable a social worker to help people more reliably, instead of harming them because of a personal need to punish or protect. Such training also guards the health of the worker in the emotional battering of case after case of trouble. One can bear to work scientifically with emotional as well as physical suffering, if one is equipped with the means of helping and can be freed from personal involvement with the problems presented. This quality in trained professional people is a solid gain from twenty-five years of concentration with psychiatric studies. Every gain has its negative aspects, however, and just when one is most sure that personal needs are no longer operative, they have subtle ways of getting back their influence upon thought and action. There are personal fears that are so much a part of the culture in which we grow up that we are not even aware of them. The fear of being too kind is as much a personal problem as is an irrational need to be kind.

Let us trace another development in the history of social work. What happened to the fear of the poor which expressed itself in the English Poor Laws, and even in the Charity Organization movement? There was fear, to begin with, that if poverty went unrelieved, as it mounted to mass proportions during the industrial revolution, no one's possessions would be safe. Then there was fear that once the community had admitted some responsibility the poor would become more demanding, instead of satisfied. Where would relief giving stop? We know the device of making relief so disagreeable that no one would seek it who could possibly do anything else. We know the "casework" answer, in that "friendly visiting" discovered resources that would not otherwise be apparent, or, at its best, really built up people so that they could do more for themselves.

The fear of spoiling people is not unrelated to fear of the demanding poor, much as its modern dress makes it seem to be the offspring of a casework principle—to foster the self-determination of the client. Psychiatric studies, however, have thrown much light on the meaning of the term, "a spoiled child." It was for long a popular notion that children and others are spoiled by having too much done for them. Now we know that the discontent, restlessness and temper outbursts characteristic of a "spoiled" person are symptoms of frustration and actually of *deprivation.* A pampered child has been robbed of his right to grow up naturally, has been frustrated in his urge to express himself and even to suffer hardship to achieve something he wants.

Modern casework, then, with its scientific understanding of the persons with whom it deals, must take account of the fact that the world is full of people who are deprived in one way or another, not always by lack of material things, and who may express their frustration by being demanding and also faultfinding toward anything that is done for them. This need not be feared any more than any other symptom. These tendencies are not made worse by liberal giving, or cured by more deprivation. The symptom is affected only when the person is built up by increasing his security, self-respect and self-confidence, and by opportunities to be active in worthwhile ways. The scientific answer, then, to this old, popular notion about spoiling people is that it is not the amount of aid or service that matters, so much as the way it is given in conjunction with the casework process of helping people to be active for themselves. To us, then, friendly giving of practical help does not preclude good casework, but is, rather, characteristic of it.

If the question, Don't you spoil people? is applied specifically to the personal service department of the National Maritime Union, the answer is that this was a particularly fortunate place to experiment with the kind of casework which need not be afraid of spoiling people. Most social agencies which believe that the healing thing for their clients is opportunity to work out something for themselves find the belief hard to make concrete because they cannot command satisfying jobs to offer, or resources for pleasant avocations for therapy. Association with a trade union was not utopia, but the Union members did have something that no social agency could offer, and which Personal Service could use in its work. In their group life in their union, seamen had opportunity for self-expression, responsibility, a chance to see how effort paid in real gains, and lack of effort produced enlightening failures. This was a laboratory directly at hand, for experiment in social living, which could be vastly therapeutic for troubled individuals. What Personal Service could do to save the time of the members, or relieve their anxieties, was placed in a healthy setting of their responsible participation in a group which was concerned with the welfare of all.

2. Why the Union Feared Social Workers

The Union had to make its own adjustment to having a group of professional service workers come into its hall. It could never forget, as outside middle-class women might, that a union is not a social agency, but exists for just one purpose, the protection of the economic interests of its members by the members themselves. Under conditions of conflict between the profit incentive in the shipping industry and the need of the workers for a living wage and healthful conditions of work, the Union had to be a fighting organization, demanding of its members high responsibility, courage and self-sacrifice for the good of everyone. For too long the industry had paid wages which condemned its seamen to homelessness and deprivation ashore, and it would never voluntarily change those conditions. Men who now earned enough to marry, because they were organized to secure contracts and enforce them, were fighting for their homes and families. They tried to educate recruits who were unused to taking responsibility in a democratic organization, and to discipline those who proved themselves unfit for responsibility. The Union officers had some fear that professional social workers would weaken the morale of the most responsible by catering to the wants of the irresponsible. The Union was at one with the United Seamen's Service in wanting the loan fund to be used for genuine emergencies, which were not contributed to by avoidable negligence on the part of the applicants.

The personal service workers were at first confused by what seemed like a different standard from that of their profession. They came prepared to shed any middle-class prejudices they might have, and, according to their professional code, to be endlessly accepting of behavior which might not coincide with their personal standards. They had been taught in professional school to be "non-judgmental," and to work with people where they were. They had, however, been accustomed to work with individuals, and their training had not prepared them to see the group mores behind the man at the desk, mores which influenced him although he might be expressing a revolt from his group in what he said. In the Union, the group was close and vocal, and a social worker could not easily miss what it had to say. Professional workers who prided themselves upon not "imposing" a standard learned, after an initial shock of realization, that the standard here was neither theirs, nor the alien standard of people from a different way of life, but the standard of the seaman's own working group. This new understanding came most clearly around the issues of discrimination and alcoholism.

The Union had been organized, and had won its gains, on the principle of unity of all seamen, without discrimination for nationality, creed or color. It sent men to jobs in strict rotation, by the time of their registration, and compelled shipping companies to accept the qualified men sent. Union members knew that, regardless of their southern or nationality prejudices,

they had to accept as a shipmate whoever was assigned with them and treat him as a Union brother.
Sometimes a man would confide in a personal service
worker who seemed sympathetic, and say that he had
refused an assignment to a job when he saw that he
would have to room with a Negro, and was therefore in
need of a loan until he could get another. The personal
service department, in a union whose wartime duty it
was to man ships, and whose very existence depended
on unity and full human rights for all members, could
not contradict union policy by giving loans under
such circumstances.

The treatment of men who could not control their
drinking was another problem. They were, of course,
caught in emergencies more frequently than others,
perhaps robbed of their pay in waterfront saloons,
perhaps injured or ill as a result of being unable to
take care of themselves. They were often very appeal-
ing on the basis of their own or their families' need. The
Union was not moralistic about drinking, but it could
not afford to ignore loss of responsibility from whatever
cause. In picturesque language, Union officials said
that they did not want Personal Service to run a "gas
hound's paradise."*

Social workers were confused at first, because they
regarded excessive drinking as a disease, and noted
that one of the signs of war nerves was furious drinking
to avoid being alone with frightful images of the death
of men at sea. They tried to get men with a "hang-
over" after a bout of drinking to see a psychiatrist
at the Medical Center, and perhaps to consider Rest

* Definitions: Alcohol is "gas." To get drunk is to be "gassed up."
A man who drinks too much is a "gas hound."

Center treatment until they were fit to ship out. More often than not, the men refused anything but a loan, for a room in which they could sleep for twenty-four hours and for some hot food before they shipped again. Perhaps they could not trust themselves with the letdown of even a brief respite from the grim business of keeping the ships moving in wartime. The leaders of the Union were heartily in favor of all that could be done for men who were heroically keeping on their feet. They only objected to cultivating the weaknesses of the irresponsible.

It was hard to know if refusal of medical care meant a high sense of responsibility or a guilty reaction to weakness. Perhaps it would result in a more severe break at sea, out of reach of medical help, where the man would endanger the lives of others. It took sound psychiatric judgment to deal with these cases, one by one, relieving guilt about drinking, explaining how others are affected by war strain, urging medical advice or at least one interview with a psychiatrist. Beyond that, however, the personal service workers came to realize, out of their own mistakes, that the problem of alcoholism goes beyond casework help, which depends for its effectiveness upon a man's having ego strength to participate in his own rehabilitation. It is a symptom which may reflect a weak personality, but which goes back to social conditions, and is not reachable, except in relatively few cases, without much preventive treatment in the social group. Among seamen, such alcoholism as there was was directly traceable to long periods of emotional strain and deprivation at sea, loneliness, having no place to meet friends except in waterfront saloons. The men, even confirmed alcoholics, were sober at their work, but drank ashore, some of them to excess, to work off accumulated tension and boredom which other workers dissipate by drinking spread more evenly over their lives, or by other ways of relieving tension. The personal service workers came to respect greatly the way the Union members regarded prevention of excessive drinking as concomitant with securing for themselves better conditions ashore as well as at sea. The maintenance of self-respect, and responsibility was of the highest value in strengthening morale in the whole group, and that, in turn, was of the greatest assistance to the weaker members. Much as some needed psychiatric care (which it was almost impossible for a worker who must earn his living at sea to get over a long period), what the crew members did for each other was beyond calculation. Casework could not, in this setting, isolate individuals from their own group which imposed its own standards and furnished its own correctives for many of their maladjustments.

3. Are Clients People?

Does it weaken clients to have things done for them? When the question is put in that form, it might be well to test it by substituting the word, *people*, for clients. Once we do that, we can think of a host of instances in which the question becomes absurd. Who feels weaker because he consults a travel bureau to plan a trip, even though he does not pay for the service? Who objects to asking a traffic policeman, or a service station, for direction, rather than hunting for the road himself? Is a banker who has his chauffeur drive him to the office rendered dangerously helpless? How about us-

ing barber shops and beauty parlors, being waited on
at table, buying clothes ready-made and food ready-
cooked? A few examples are enough to show that this
concept is essentially a piece of class thinking, from the
side of the classes which are privileged to have as
much service as they want because they can pay for
it. It might be said for the banker that riding comfortably to work is saving his energies, to use his brain for
work of greater importance than coping with traffic
problems. So might everyone who buys service cite the
fact of being busy with other responsibilities of social
value. Are people in the client group, however, not
supposed to have brains to use elsewhere, if they are
relieved of some small task? Are they just factory or
farm "hands" (how significant of attitudes words
are!)? Of course we know what the proverb says that
Satan does with idle hands. Someone once argued for
the ten-hour workday on the basis that shortened hours
would give workers too much time for "conniving."
Are clients a different kind of human being from the
so-called leisure class, about whom the allegation,
"Some people won't work" would be merely amusing?
Is leaning on a shovel a more sinister symptom than
leaning on a golf club?

One who works for a membership organization of
any sort has to rid himself quickly of any class concept
that clients are not *people* in the same sense as everyone else. They are busy people, laden with responsibilities, and any service by which they can avoid un-
necessary loss of time and energy is valuable to them.
They have not been made dependent, usually, by being brought up to believe that service from a servant
class is their due, neither have they, usually, been

forced to be the passive, obedient recipients of charity. A casework service using professional skills to build up the activity of the person where it counts most in his life-situation has no reason to fear doing little services which are the visible tokens of a relationship of cordial helpfulness.

Personal Service at NMU found emotionally dependent people, as every social agency does. In coming to the loan service, they often used a request for money symbolically, to express their wish for an enveloping protection and care. It is no answer to such a need, on the part of people whom life has damaged badly, to say that they show too little maturity, and should be eliminated at application. It is a better answer, while expecting no miracles of rehabilitation, to say that we take people where they are, and through the small concrete service which it was possible for them to ask, bring them some of the feeling of being welcomed and understood, and some stimulation to find ways of helping themselves.

The two cases which follow are examples of how fear of spoiling people, or freedom from it, have a direct bearing upon the casework process itself.

4. A Woman Who Might Become Dependent

Jane Cummings had been referred to a private family service agency, by letter, from the social service department of Eastlake Hospital on November 6, 1940. Miss Cummings, who was forty-two years old, had been a ward patient there from August 28th to October 1st, with a diagnosis of bronchial asthma. She had been given four weeks' care at a convalescent home, and this had been extended three more weeks by the kind-

ness of a friend who paid her expenses. There was no
further extension possible, nor any other available institution, yet she did not seem well enough to return to
work, nor did she have a home or means to live until
she was well. The medical social worker made the referral to a private agency, rather than an application
for public relief, because of special circumstances:
Miss Cummings had never married, and was the main
support of a widowed mother and invalid brother until
she became ill two years ago. She had earned a very
adequate salary as buyer for a department store, and
was so capable a person that it was expected that,
with favorable conditions for her recovery, she would
soon be self-supporting again. She was so disturbed
about being dependent that a referral to public assistance would hopelessly complicate her convalescence.
She needed casework help in making an emotional adjustment to somewhat reduced activity, and in re-
establishing her sense of competence and her courage
to take up living again. There was no possibility of her
making her home with relatives during this interval,
because of illness and financial difficulties in the
homes of her married sisters.

Miss Cummings was given an appointment by the
Family Society, by letter, for November 14th, and
when she did not receive this in time was given another for November 22nd. On that day Miss Cummings came in a half hour late. The following is taken
from the case record:

"She was dressed in black which accentuated
her sickly pallor and sunken eyes. She was breathing heavily, and talked in a dull, tired voice. She

began by saying we probably knew all about her from the hospital. We said we knew a little, but would she tell us how things looked to her. She took a deep breath, and said she must obtain a place to live, immediately, as she must leave the Convalescent Home in three days. She has made a special trip to the city to talk with us. She understands from the hospital social worker that perhaps we can find her a place to stay. She really does not know what we do here.

"We said we would be glad to help if we could, and asked what her plans were. She said she would not like to stay with her married sister, Mrs. Nolan, since her husband is not working and is suffering from arthritis. She conveyed the impression that she thought we would be able to place her in a room immediately. We explained that we had only a list of rooms, and could not make the actual search for her. We made this clear since Miss C. seemed to feel that she was relieved of this responsibility by coming to the office, and expressed her disappointment by becoming somewhat hostile. We said that placing people was not primarily our function, although we took up the matter in connection with other problems. We realized what a burden it was to go around looking for rooms, especially if she was not well.

"Miss C. began to talk of her physical condition. She said that if she were strong she would not have to be in this position at all, and certainly she could take the responsibility of looking for a room. She immediately rejected the suggestion that some member of her family might help her find a place,

saying that they had their own problems. She broke
down and began to sniffle, although she did not
cry. She controlled herself enough to say that she
never expected that she would come to accepting
charity. All her life she has been independent, but
now she has reached the end of her rope. She
seemed to obtain satisfaction in relating that she
was referred here some time ago, but when the executive wrote her a letter she tore it up, and ignored the appointment, although she was in great
financial straits at the time, early in her illness.
She showed fear in her face and voice when she
questioned whether we intended to investigate her
former place of employment. When she was assured that we would not without her permission,
she sighed with relief, and said she would never
want them to know that she had fallen so low, after
being in an executive position. At this point, after
further reassurance, we changed the subject,
thinking Miss C. was too disturbed to discuss past
experiences or future plans. We began to make
telephone calls to locate rooms for Miss C. to visit.
She was given an appointment for Monday (this
was Friday), by which time she will need money
for room rent. She left, saying we would never
know how hard it was for her to come here, and
expressing gratitude for our kindness and understanding. She expects to repay every penny when
she gets to work in a month or so.

"Diagnostic Impressions: It is our feeling that a
good deal of money and treatment is indicated, in
view of Miss C's highly emotional state. We did
not press referral to the Department of Public

Welfare, since it was so difficult for her to accept assistance from anyone. We briefly mentioned it in a casual way, but Miss C. immediately refused to consider it. It may be necessary at some time to prepare her for a possible referral. However, if upon study we find Miss C. so emotionally disturbed that it is impossible for her to accept DPW at any point, we may be obligated to carry on with her on a relief basis as well as for treatment.

"(Monday) Miss C. came in an hour late, looking haggard and worn, and saying that she had had a frightful experience looking for rooms. In addition to being limited to climbing not more than one flight of stairs, she found many things wrong with the rooms she saw. (She gave the impression of being quite critical.) She was in panic because she had left the Convalescent Home, and must find something before night. In desperation, she said she hoped we would know somebody who would take her in, not just depend on our files. She feels she has lost all she has gained in the last weeks, and knows she can't think straight, and stupidly goes around in circles.

"We said everyone feels that way when under strain. Suppose she should think that if worse came to worst she *might* stay with her sister for a few days till she could find a place. She protested against this, but we thought it was to show us that this could not be considered as a permanent plan, and she really seemed relieved to think that at the worst she would not be out on the street. We spent a good deal of time looking up new addresses and telephoning, and then Miss C. produced some newspaper ads. She complained that $3 which we had budgeted for a room was not enough to get a decent place, and because of her emotional tension we raised it to $4 and gave her the money, so that she could make a payment when she found the room. She seemed to feel more confidence in her ability to find something after this. She left with profuse thanks, and seemingly accepted the job of finding the room as hers, while being conscious that she could not get along without the help we were giving."

The following is a summary of the remainder of a rather long record:

Then followed a period of several weeks in which Miss Cummings telephoned frequently until she had found a permanent room near her sister's home where her mother was living, and came in regularly for her allowance for food and room rent. After a while, she began to make some contacts looking toward employment, though she had periodic relapses into illness, and the caseworker noted that she seemed to resist the idea of a full-time job. The prognosis for her return to complete independence seemed doubtful to the caseworker. The following history came out gradually:

Miss Cummings had devoted her whole life to her family, even to helping the children of her married sisters through school. She had allowed herself few pleasures, outside of some social contacts in connection with her work, and had been proud of her ability to meet every family emergency. When she became ill, it was a major blow to her to realize that her family cared nothing for her, except for what they could get out of her. She lost confidence in herself as a person, and could find only a dubious satisfaction in being taken care of, a role which filled her with shame at her own worthlessness.

Interviews with the caseworker, occurring naturally as she came in for her allowance, gradually gave her a different point of view about herself and her relationship to her family. She was accepted by the caseworker as a person who had a right to the things in life that other people had. She began to see that her need to give to her family had been an unconscious buying of a place in their affections, and that she had even forced benefits upon them. She realized that they had not been as demanding as she had liked to think. She saw how their own problems were real obstacles to their giving her the all-embracing kind of care she had longed to receive from someone. She still saw her family often, but began, more and more, to live her own life. In six months she was working at a job which she found for herself as saleswoman, less satisfying in many ways than her old one, but with much less strain. Being freed from her need to contribute to her family as excessively as before, she was content with a smaller salary, and gave herself more rest and small pleasures than she had ever before allowed herself. A review of the record shows something like a temperature chart of improvement and regression during these six months. It is noticeable that the slumps corresponded exactly with suggestions of withdrawal of relief, or referral to the Department of Public Welfare.

COMMENT: Miss Cummings' caseworker was evidently a person skilled in the use of a professional relationship to bring a distressed woman through a trying period with a definite change in her orientation toward living. One does not know how familiar the worker was with the studies in psychosomatic medicine which have thrown much light on the emotional aspects of bronchial asthma—the kind of fear-ridden personality which is predisposed to it, and the use the patient makes of the disease when intolerable pressures from an over-driving conscience make it imperative to obtain rest and care in some acceptable way. Even if she was without such knowledge (which would give clues more rapidly), the caseworker could have estimated the trauma it was to the patient to have the frightening experience of finding a place to live after a long period of hospital care had convinced her that she was seriously ill, and after losing all the props which doing for others had placed under her self-esteem. The caseworker tried valiantly to locate rooms, and quite skillfully drew Miss C. into taking responsibility for visiting them, but her fear that Miss C's dependency would become a permanent pattern led her constantly to take the precaution of warning Miss C. that the agency might not be able to go on like this.

Even from the first interviews, it is evident that the caseworker alternately gave Miss C. a bit of security that she would be understood and helped, and then took it away by hints about referral. Miss C. was left doubtful of being either accepted or rejected, and even her expressions of gratitude may reflect this uncertainty. She was given too little rent money for a room in a city in 1940, and this complicated the search, but the caseworker seems to have to justify to the agency her giving more, by placing the onus on Miss C's disturbed state. All through the part of the record which we have summarized, the caseworker gave and drew back so continually that Miss C., in fear of being deserted just as she was getting on her feet, had to relapse into illness again. Miss C's first suggestions of employment were seized too quickly, and pushed too fast, with the result that Miss C. had to get her bearings in another attack of asthma before she could resume her own effort. Both Miss C. and her caseworker had qualities favorable to a good outcome, and much skillful casework was done, but the adjustment took longer because the caseworker could not free herself from fear that the agency would be imposed upon, nor avoid inspiring the patient with the fear that she would be abandoned.

5. A Young Couple Needs Money

Another example shows that when subsistence needs are urgent casework service cannot ignore them. An agency is, on the contrary, in a more favorable position to do good casework if it has some money to use in a way that is consistent with a client's self-respect. This case was not complicated by the worker's conflict about giving.

The personal service department of the National Maritime Union received a telephone call in May, 1945, from Nicolas Montez, a twenty-three-year-old seaman who had become ineligible for membership in the Union when he had qualified for a third mate's license a year before. He wanted advice, and turned to Personal Service which had helped him on a winter day when he had pawned his only overcoat to help his family (in which were five younger brothers and sisters) through a crisis of illness. Personal Service had given a small loan then, and three months later made it possible for him to stave off an eviction, while his mother was ill in bed, and he would have to wait a month for his pay at Officers' Training School.

Now Nicolas had a nice wife, and a little home of his own, and he had been very happy until his wife became ill. They were without savings to meet expenses until his allotment could be received—in two weeks if he should sail immediately. Could Personal Service tell him where he could borrow a minimal sum? There seemed to be no loan agency which would give credit to a seaman, and loans from United Seamen's Service were restricted to unlicensed seamen. The caseworker suggested consulting a family agency. Mr. Montez was afraid of social agencies. He said he would rejoin the Union and sail as bosun, the next lower rating to his present one. His taking a demotion seemed a little strange. Was it pique, or hope that by this means he would become eligible for a personal service loan?

Two days later, Nicolas came in really desperate. Last night his wife was so ill that he was frightened and called an ambulance. The doctor who came said that she need not go to the hospital, but was exhausted, and a cold had given her some fever. She must have complete rest for two weeks at least. She had been working in an office, and going to college three nights a week, and worry had taken her last bit of energy. Meanwhile his parents had an impossible load to carry, with one child sick and the father's pay just not enough for seven people. Nicolas felt he must help them too. He needed money at once, but had rejoined the Union, and would have to wait his turn for a job, and then two weeks before an allotment could reach his wife.

At this point, the caseworker asked Brother Montez why he was taking a job at lower rating than third mate, for which he was qualified. He explained without hesitation that he had felt very nervous since a trip last fall when he thought he sighted a submarine when he was on lookout. He started to run to give the alarm, but he could not move or speak, and was shaking all over. He believes now it was only a porpoise, but submarines are still a terrible menace, and he has never recovered his nerve. He goes into a panic at any loud noise, eats and sleeps poorly, is afraid to go home lest he cannot control himself. Last trip, just before they reached port, he had what the purser said was an epileptic fit. That worries him because he used to have attacks as a child, before he came to this country from Puerto Rico, but he thought he was cured. He *must* make a trip now because he needs money so badly, but he cannot stand the responsibility of being an officer. He knows that any job on a ship is a responsible one, but not in quite the same way as when other people's lives hang on an officer's doing the right thing.

The caseworker suggested that the rest centers were established for just such health problems as his, and that he might also have some treatment there for his nerves. He agreed that he needs rest, but that will not restore his wife's health, or relieve their worry about rent which is due in a few days. They cannot bear to lose their little apartment, recently set up, which is to them a symbol of building a life of their own. Formerly, both of them were supporting their parental families, and saw no future. He has just persuaded his wife

to let her brothers and sisters do their share in supporting their mother.

It was Friday. If he could have a few days to take
his wife to the park, and see if she would pick up
strength, perhaps they could together find some way
out. He was sure she would understand the caseworker's point that it was important for him to get treatment now, even with all the other factors. He expressed
his confidence in his wife by saying, "Whatever she says
goes." He agreed to come back Monday for referral to
Medical Center for a thorough examination, for he understood the caseworker's reminder that the purser was
not exactly a specialist.

COMMENT: Brother Montez had a plan, and a source of
strength in his confidence in his wife. Gaining the time
to work it out depended on money for food until Monday. As small a sum as $6 would be enough. Other-
wise, dependence on relatives who were already
desperate, guilt, worry, recriminations perhaps, might
lead to throwing away the whole idea of medical treatment. This is what we mean when we say that when
money is needed there is no substitute for it. As was
shown later, this family would sacrifice greatly to help
each other, but sometimes pressure of need is so com-
pelling that the future (represented by a chance to get
well) has to be sacrificed to immediate necessities.
There was no question in the mind of the personal service worker that an investment of six dollars today was
required to make any constructive plan work. She made
it a loan because Nicolas insisted, but with the understanding that he should not pay it back until he was well
able to do so. She did not hedge about with uncertain-

ties her statement that when the extent of the problem was known some plan could be worked out. United Seamen's Service loans existed for a temporary emergency, public welfare, if the time needed for restoration proved to be more than two or three weeks. There was no need on her part to impress Brother Montez with how much was being done for him, or with the unwisdom of his expecting too much. It was important to get him to working on his own and his wife's health problems without being paralyzed by fear. She did not plan with him beyond the week-end, because she respected his desire to think it out with his wife, and because she wanted him to feel that the key to any plan was an accurate medical diagnosis. He was ready for that, if he could bring his wife's thinking along with his.

Nicolas returned on Monday. His wife went back to work today, though she is not really fit. She wants him to get medical treatment. The caseworker again emphasized to him that if his wife is not well any plan made should include her too. The week-end brought another blow, an income tax bill from three years ago, when he had paid $45 thinking it was for the year, instead of only one quarter. He must pay at once. His sister-in-law would lend him her savings, but that is not enough. His wife gets back pay today, enough to take care of the rent, and they will eat at the homes of relatives till next pay day. He will try everywhere today to raise the tax money, and also go for a medical examination.

Nicolas was not heard from for ten days, when he telephoned for an appointment. He had been sent to the hospital for injections to control seizures, and was com-

ing home for the week-end on a hospital pass. He came
to the personal service department reporting a gain in
weight of five pounds. He had been terribly under-
weight. He is having encephalograms, and other tests,
and may be discharged in a week. The family situation
is still critical, but Nicolas has realistically separated
the problem of the parental families from that of his
primary obligation to his wife. In his father's home a
brother will be earning soon. He discussed with the
caseworker the procedure of application to the Department of Public Welfare, if supplementation is needed
for them in an emergency.

The income tax was paid after his sister-in-law gave
him money she had saved for her vacation. His wife
got only $8 pay this week, because of time lost for sick-
ness, and this will be used up for carfares and food.
It costs her $1.50 a day to live. They are most worried
about payments on furniture for which they owe $363
and have contracted to pay $63 a month. They have
had one extension of time already. The personal service
worker offered to call the company for him, but Nicolas
preferred to call them himself. He showed the account
book, and the caseworker included in the budget she
worked out with him $13 to hold the account till he
could get to work. $24 was the supplementary sum
agreed upon for his needs and his wife's for the next
two weeks.

Nicolas came in in September of the same year to report that he had been given medicine which he took
for four months after he went back to work. He had
had plenty of rest and felt well until a cold had paralyzed certain nerves of his face. He was now taking
treatment at a clinic three times a week, and could not

ship out until he was entirely recovered. He would have subsistence money from the company while he was under treatment, about $24 a week, but his wife was ill, and without her wages they could not manage. (The caseworker suggested that his wife come in when she was able, and she did a few days later, to talk over her health problem.) Nicolas was concerned that repayment of his loans had just not been possible. He had kept up furniture payments so that they did not have to give up their home, and he can get extension of time now that he is up to date on those. A loan for one week for food and rent until subsistence would be paid seemed essential at this time.

A month later, Mrs. Montez came in, since the caseworker had said she might help her find a job less exhausting than the waitress' work she was doing now. Nicolas was well, and sailing as able-bodied seaman, a rating in which he could get a job quickly. She is worn out, having tried again to carry college courses, and a job. They have talked about her going to school full time as soon as Nicolas gets regular pay. Her own medical problem was discussed with her, and some information about clinics was given so that she could avoid the expense of going to a private physician just now. A referral letter was given. Her cousin who was with her, suggested that she does not eat enough.

Mrs. Montez said that, though he never has seizures now, she knows that her husband's susceptibility to nervous strain will always be with him. The hardships of a voyage are apt to reduce his tolerance of strain. The same day, just as he was sailing and was unable to leave the dock, Nicolas telephoned Personal Service, and was much relieved that his wife had been in and the department would stand by her till his return.

In April of the next year, Nicolas telephoned as soon as he reached the city, on his return from a trip, to say that he was repaying his loans at the cashier's office where repayments were handled.

During that summer he and his wife were both sick with a fever prevalent in their neighborhood, but he was free from seizures, and laid his improved health to his wife. "She takes such good care of me." He had tried shipping as mate once, but took a lower rating whenever he felt a sense of strain. By this time, though they had no margin for emergencies, they had worked out a plan of allotments to the credit union at the Union Hall, so that they could clean up their indebtedness and eventually, they hoped, build up a savings account.

Was this young couple "spoiled" by the help given to them?

v i. Is Diagnosis an Imposition?

1. A Bit of History

Social work got its start, as a young profession, with the publication in 1917 of Mary Richmond's *Social Diagnosis*. This book was a summation of the best that had been learned up to that time. It assumed that the social worker's contribution to the solution of the client's problem was a kind of understanding and of knowledge of social resources out of which a plan of action could be developed. As we read it through to-day we are struck by certain differences from our present thinking, notably two: Less reliance on the participation of the client and more on social evidence from interested people as to what the facts are; secondly, bringing the client into planning only when the social worker is in possession of all the relevant facts obtainable. When, after World War I, facts about mental attitudes and emotions were added to the record of behavior and events, as relevant material, social work required voluminous social histories. Out of these, it was hoped, would come direction as to what to do in the problem situation.

The publication of Virginia Robinson's *A Changing Psychology in Social Case Work*, in 1930, was another milestone in growth into a profession. It made the client the center of the process of helping him, and made his choice of material from his past the caseworker's guide to what was important to him now. It placed the dynamic of casework help in the *relationship* which developed between the client and the professional person. It was this sharing with one who was understanding, and, by professional training, more objective than the client's friends, that made it possible for the client to see his problem more clearly, and take hold of it with more courage and effectiveness.

As the years have gone on, social work theory has tended to incorporate much of both the intellectual and the feeling, or relationship, approach to the art of social casework. It has also tended to polarize to some extent around two concepts which are not opposed but are at times made to seem so. One is akin to Mary Richmond's idea of social diagnosis as the central contribution of professional social work, its unique difference from the helpfulness of neighbors and friends. The other follows from Miss Robinson's emphasis on relationship as a helping factor that must not be disturbed by the authority which is implied in a professional diagnosis. If the client is the only one, so runs this theory, who really knows himself and how he feels, he alone can diagnose his trouble and prescribe the remedies. A professional person can only be responsible for setting up and maintaining a process of helping which is use of a relationship. This relationship is made scientific by the professional worker's trained self-discipline and skill in relating the function of the social agency to the client's need. This theory, which has been called "functional" because of its emphasis upon the function of the social agency as determinative of the casework process, considers that the term and the concept of diagnosis are borrowed from medicine, and have retarded the growth of social work into a profession with its own standards and discipline.

The thinking and experience of this writer find that penetrating diagnoses and dynamic relationships in social work are not opposed but complementary. Each stresses something essential, and each, without the other, can be carried to an absurdity. If diagnosis means *seeing into* or *seeing through,* that is not possible without a relationship with the client which releases him to be himself, to explore his trouble freely because a helping person is there. To be able to do something about what one sees is no less dependent on the security and stimulation of a relationship to a professional person. On the other hand, a relationship becomes meaningful if it brings to bear on the problem not only the caseworker's warmth but light which is drawn from scientific training, and from experience in dealing with many such problems. It frees the individual from a sense of being smothered in trouble that is his alone, and lets him draw on experience that is more comprehensive than his, and more free from emotional entanglements. Diagnosis, then, is not imposing the thinking of a stranger with alien interests, but weaving together the threads that both client and caseworker draw from life and work on together.

2. Diagnosis in Short Contacts

The new kind of agency we have described, the experiment under joint operation of a social agency and a trade union, was a unique laboratory for study of diagnostic theory and methods in social work. Superficially, it may seem that one could not think in terms of adequate diagnoses in an agency working with seamen who had at most a month, and usually much less under war shipping regulations, to stay ashore. Could a relationship be maintained long enough to do anything significant with a person or his life situation under such conditions? There has been a tendency in social work to feel that such services as information-giving, making loans, finding hospital care for a wife or placement for a child, are minor services, not worth the time of a caseworker skilled in problems of emotional adjustment, such as have held the prestige position as social casework.

One reason for believing that this form of practice calls for casework skills of the highest order is that diagnosis, in its literal sense of *seeing through*, must be focused quickly upon the most essential parts of the problem, and those with which something constructive can be done immediately. Treatment must be related to what the person can pick up and work with himself, after he has left the caseworker. An estimate of the applicant's ability to take hold of his problem has to be as accurate as possible, and made on far less data than is available in a leisurely acquaintance. The relationship must be established with less delay than is usual when an applicant goes to an agency he is not sure he can trust. The caseworker must use all available knowledge of the industry, and of conditions to which the seafarer is exposed, to make an appraisal of what the man's resources are in that environment. This is in addition to what is observed and learned from the interview with the particular person. A social diagnosis in a short-contact agency, then, is not a snap judgment, nor is it necessarily superficial. If it cannot explore a person's whole life it must see with even more clarity the limited piece of work that can be done in a limited time.

What did the wartime experience of a social agency-trade union personal service department indicate about the possibilities of using diagnostic skills in a brief contact? Two examples of typical cases may show what was involved, both as to skill in focusing quickly on the main problem, and in establishing a professional relationship which would inspire confidence.

3. Two Examples:
a. A Request for Information

The first case is an example of the very simplest service, a request for information from a seaman's brother, while the seaman, Michael Harrigan, was at sea. Michael's wife, from whom he had been separated for some time, had just died, leaving two children of school age and a baby whom Michael had not acknowledged as his child. Michael had made an allotment from his wages, but not to his wife. He had it sent for the support of his mother, and, since she could not read or write, sent it in the name of the wife of his brother, the applicant. The latter wanted to know two things, now that the Department of Welfare had taken charge of the children: How he could get custody of them, not including the baby, and give them a home with his own eight children, and whether his wife had involved him in a serious liability, since she had signed a paper, when she was interviewed by the Department of Welfare, promising to pay $40 a month for the children's care out of Michael's allotment.

The information asked for could be given almost automatically: that the father was legally responsible for his children, and a plan for their support would have to be worked out between him and the Department of Welfare; also, that if the allotment ceased the uncle could not be held responsible. What did the caseworker see in the situation that called for a use of professional skill in addition to simple giving of information?

The caseworker saw a man in his forties, a railroad worker, taking vacation time to clear up his brother's affairs and ready, if he was permitted to do so, to take his brother's two children home with him. He said if he could feed eight, two more would not make much difference, and he liked the kids. It was not possible to tell how much he was influenced by desire to keep Michael's money contribution in the family. The caseworker could have handled the information by the negative statement, "You cannot do anything until your brother returns." Instead, she found one point at which she could use her trained understanding in the few minutes at her disposal. She stressed Michael's responsibility, and his right to be consulted in such a way as to make him the center of the group concerned about the children, and not a troublesome detail in the margin. In discussion, she alleviated Mr. Harrigan's criticism of his wife's action by showing that there was really nothing to fear. She tried to prepare Mr. Harrigan for a clear-thinking family conference on his brother's return, instead of a confused one in which each of the adults might be fighting the others to defend his own rights in the situation.

Within the limits of this practical problem the caseworker saw what difficulties might be present in family interrelationships, and was able to focus on one, Michael's place in the family picture, which she could possibly influence, in the way she gave the information asked for, to create a better mental climate in which the family could discuss the future of the children. If anyone feels that this was not casework because the worker did not know enough to make judgments about the situation, or give any social treatment, the answer is that of course she did not know enough to take charge of the disposition of the children. She did not even know the personalities of Michael and his brother and brother's wife. However, her knowledge of social relationships did tell her how to create a favorable base for a solution which the people concerned could use if they were able, and it was she who sensed that in the situation itself there were as many possibilities for distorted as for healthy attitudes toward the children. Her very simple form of social treatment, then, entered into the situation with a clarification which was different in quality from just giving information about the legal rulings which guide the Department of Welfare.

b. A Request for a Loan

Another example is associated with a request for a loan: Peter Royal was assigned to a ship as chief cook, and was to sail in a day or two. He said he had never asked help of the personal service department before, but rent must be paid, and all the money he had to leave his wife would barely cover the family's food until his first allotment check would reach them in two weeks. He explained that he would have had savings, except that his wife had been ailing for about a year, and her doctor's bills had been costing him at least ten dollars a week. In answer to a question, he said he did not know what was the matter with her, and he doubted if the doctor did. He did not know the doctor, who had been recommended by his wife's church friends. There were no symptoms except a terrible weakness. She would try to sit up, and fall back exhausted. He said he had three girls who got along with the housework somehow, with the help of women from the church who came in every day.

It was obvious that this man was accustomed to planning for himself. He had asked only a loan, and the personal service department could give the equivalent of half a month's rent, in case there were no other way of holding off the threat of an eviction, at a time when landlords were taking advantage of a terrific demand for apartments. It was likely that Mr. Royal did not know of anything else that Personal Service could do for him. What could be offered?

The caseworker formulated the problem to herself in this fashion: The wife's illness, to have lasted so long, must be either a late stage of some debilitating disease, or the exhaustion of a mental or emotional illness. If it were the latter, the physician might have no understanding of the case, yet it would be a delicate matter to suggest a change, particularly as the interest of the woman's friends was involved. There was no way to get a psychiatrist to visit the home, and Personal Service workers were not able to leave the office. A family service agency might send someone to see the patient, and try to get more data on the medical problem. How would Mr. Royal understand the need of a visit?

The Personal Service worker asked him if he had thought of the possibility that his wife's illness might be due to some deep anxiety rather than physical disease. She said that she asked that, not to intrude into his affairs but because doctors who are experts in diseases of the body are sometimes quite baffled by a nervous illness. She wondered if there were any other kind of medical care that his wife might need. Mr. Royal said that he had thought of that also, but he did not know how to get a specialist who would understand this kind of illness. The caseworker discussed with him the difficulties, but suggested that a family service agency might help to find resources, particularly as he was sailing so soon. With his active interest, the worker called the district office of the nearest Family agency, making her statement of the case in the man's presence a means of further clarification for him. He accepted gratefully an appointment for the same afternoon. The worker let his financial problem rest where he had placed it, with the personal service department, so that he could go to the Family agency free from the embarrassment (which would have been for him acute) of asking for money elsewhere than in his Union hall where he felt he belonged.

The outcome was that when Mr. Royal stopped at home to tell his wife about his appointment, she wanted to go with him. In view of her extreme fatigue, he dissuaded her for this time, but a few days later the Family Service visitor had a long talk with Mrs. Royal in her home. There were several of these, followed by such marked improvement that she was able to resume care of her home and children. There was much that came out about a complicated family situation, in which Mrs. Royal periodically found herself unable to bear any more and retreated into illness. Some adjustments were made that relieved the strain somewhat, and the help she got from talking it out with someone brought her through the period of stalemate and back to her usual state of fair health. Some months later she was still well, and Mr. Royal, when he came to repay his loan, sought out the Personal Service worker to thank her for referring him to help that "really saved my home."

Here was a single interview in which a request was met, but diagnostic thinking revealed another problem which the man had no resources for solving. The referral was made in the hope of gaining more information for diagnosis than the Personal Service worker could obtain in an office interview, but, as it happened, resulted in the needed adjustment of the situation. From the point of view which we are taking, this carefully worked out referral, based on a diagnostic review of possibilities, was a casework service, and a first step in social treatment.

4.   Who Makes the Diagnosis?

We began our discussion with the question, Is diagnosis an imposition? We have traced briefly two theories of the place of diagnosis in social casework: one that it is essential to any attempt to deal with problems of individuals and families and constitutes the outstanding professional contribution to their solution, and the other that diagnosis is a hang-over from medical practice and is harmful to the helping relationship which is the core of social casework. We have taken the position that *both* a clear diagnosis and a sound relationship of helpfulness are essential, and are in reality inseparable. The two examples so far given have been of the simplest forms of diagnostic thinking, such as may occur in a single interview and in a short-contact agency. We have not yet come to grips with the possibility that there may be circumstances in which diagnoses are either irrelevant or a hindrance to the client's working out his own solution to his problem.

In recent years social workers have become sensitized to the unsoundness of doing more than the client asks or wants. We have learned to see that sometimes a service is contributed out of the caseworker's, not the client's, estimate of its appropriateness. Some agencies set up procedures for having the client define, after explanation of the agency's function, what he wants it to do for him, and they do not consider it sound to prepare him to accept a service for which he is not ready to state a request. On this basis, persuading Philip Keene (Chapter IV, Section 4) to join a credit union and to go to a canteen for seamen would have been imposing on him a caseworker's idea of what he needed. Suggesting that Mr. Royal might try to find out the nature of his wife's illness, when he had asked only for a loan might also be thought of as presuming upon the agency's being in a position to give money to offer other services he might not want.

A theory of social work which goes back to the common experiences of social living to test the soundness of its procedures finds no reason to place the initiative either entirely on the client or entirely on the caseworker. Both share in taking the lead, or follow the lead of the other, according to the expertness which each has, and the nature of the problem. Mr. Royal might not know the forms that emotional illness may take, but his judgment whether the ideas advanced by the caseworker were applicable to his wife's condition was an equally definite contribution to a plan of action. His initiative had been taken in asking for a loan, which was his only way of keeping his wife from being seriously disturbed by the landlord while he was away at sea earning more money. His plan was only to keep the situation from becoming worse, but the caseworker's contribution made possible an improvement in it which created the difference from what he could accomplish alone, or with the advice of his wife's friends. Is there reason to suppose that it is more "professional" to withhold help which a person has no way of securing for himself?

5. Diagnoses Gone Astray

These instances seem fairly obvious, but aren't there others in which a caseworker might well create new problems by giving a diagnosis which is remote from the comprehension of the client, and unrelated to anything he can use in planning? The following examples may be extreme, but present elements which are not uncommon in this writer's experience. They happen to be selected from medical social work, not because such instances occur more often in that setting but because the realities of physical illness make practical remedies more clearly necessary than in some forms of casework, and hence the principle involved is more easy to discern. The caseworkers in the two examples which follow were graduates of schools of social work which emphasize the influence of the unconscious functioning of the mind on human behavior.

A young wife, nineteen years old, with a seven months old baby, had been referred to a hospital social service department from a medical clinic because she was undernourished. Her story was that she and her husband had had a terrible time in finding a place to live, and had finally had to take a janitor's job to get an apartment. The pay was only $45 a month in cash, and she supposed the owner expected the wife to do most of the work while the husband had another job. She was not strong enough for this, and her husband had not been able to find anything else to combine with the duties which this job required. They had had to buy furniture on credit, and payments took most of what the man earned. To eat she had had to go to her mother, and her husband to his folks. She knew that neither of them got what they should have, but her mother was on relief, and could do no more for them, except to help her care for the baby.

The caseworker saw, as the focus of the problem, that this young couple was too dependent on their parents. She asked the young wife if this was not so. The patient did not return for another appointment.

Another instance concerns the rehabilitation of a man in his forties who had had his leg amputated because of an infected knee. He had done unskilled work, but with his wife's earnings this childless couple had lived rather comfortably. The man had shown the usual reactions to the loss of a part of his body, insecurity, fear of trying to use crutches, or (later) an artificial limb, fear that his wife would be shocked when she saw his stump, and that he would lose her affection. The social worker at the hospital saw him regularly over a period of months, first when he was under ward care and then when he came to the outpatient clinic for treatments. She talked with him at length about his feelings about his leg, and about his relationship to his wife. It seemed to take an endless time for him to get over his fears of going on the street alone, and to reach a point where plans could be made for his getting some kind of work.

The medical social worker had identified the man's major problem as that of psychosexual inadequacy, of which he was made acutely aware by the loss of his leg. The hope that talking about it, bringing it to full consciousness, would act as *catharsis* of his emotions, so that he would eventually feel adequate to take a job, did not materialize in the months of contact with the social worker. The man's wife, who had carried the whole support of the home, showed signs of impatience as time went on, and the man seemed more depressed and uncertain, rather than more free.

In both these instances, the social caseworker had been trained to look for problems in the unconscious, rather than in the conscious struggle of the person to deal with the facts of life confronting him. In the case of the young couple, the impossiblity of getting decent housing for any sum they could afford had led the man to become involved in a confining but inadequate job, and had resulted in malnutrition for the whole family. These stubborn facts could not be dealt with by a diagnosis which identified the major problem as an unconscious desire for dependence on their parents, who, after all, were their only resource for food. This young couple, who, possibly, *were* immature, could have been worked with together, to strengthen their family tie while they tackled together the serious problem of how to get enough food and a place to live. The medical social service department which first saw the wife might have seen that a family agency could best do this casework service while the medical agency guided the wife in carrying out diet recommendations. This diagnosis of needs would then have led to the kind of referral or cooperative arrangement which would serve the family best, and a continuing process of diagnosis would have followed through the steps that this young couple might take to find a better solution. It would not be that their emotional needs would be ignored, for their whole relationship to a caseworker would show what balance they had worked out between dependence and independence, and a good caseworker would all along be giving support and encouragement, as well as stimulation to do their best for themselves. A relevant and truly helpful diagnosis, however, would focus on the problem which they could work on themselves.

Similarly, the crippled man whose energies had been centered excessively upon himself by his illness and the loss of his leg, needed help most of all to restore him to the stream of normal living. He needed to be convinced that he could still do things and hold his own with other men, not only in earning money, but as a person in his own family. In contrast to a diagnosis related to his overcoming his handicap to whatever extent was possible, the social worker at the hospital looked for a problem in his unconscious mind, and fixed upon his fear of losing his wife's love, a fear of which he had shown some indications, as is quite usual in these cases. While she was trying to bring this fear into full consciousness, she was keeping the patient's attention centered on himself and on his weakness and feeling of inferiority rather than on his strengths. She was even creating a marital problem, as the patient developed a relationship to the social worker and the wife was more and more left to the role of wage earner for the family. If the social worker had not been preoccupied with the diagnosis which she had been trained to see and which interested her most, she could have worked with the man to develop his ability to walk, and to plan actively for some occupation. She could have strengthened the relationship between the man and his wife by keeping the wife close to the rehabilitation plans, and by making much of achievements for which the man could feel that his wife would be proud of him. She would have made full use of her knowledge of emotional life as each step of the treatment plans evoked feelings which would play a real part in the man's capacity to go ahead with confidence in himself.

These two instances remind us that a diagnosis may repel a client in need of help, or actually create new problems by a focus on something which is a passing or incidental factor, something that the client is not conscious of and cannot use in his own efforts to solve his problem. Because this question is of vital importance to an understanding of the role of diagnosis in social work, I am presenting a longer example in which, for lack of essential data, a clear estimate could not be made of how much a patient could be expected to do for himself, or in what direction help for him would have to be sought. The tragic note in the following case is the loss of time, two and a half years at the most critical period in a boy's life, during which treatment by exploration of his unconscious mind was tried and abandoned, while the essential problem remained unknown.

6.   Capacity and Needs Unknown

Harry Wicks was fourteen when he first met a social worker at the hospital where he had been under treatment for diabetes ever since he was five years old. A study of all juvenile diabetic cases brought him to the attention of Miss A. who sat down with him in the clinic to ask him sympathetically why it was that he had never been able to follow his diet consistently. She said she was not going to scold him (he had probably had enough of that), but could they together try to see what the trouble was? Harry's eyes filled with tears, and he responded rather readily to a plan for regular interviews. He placed his difficulty, in the first talk, on his being teased by his second younger brother, Mike, who eats bread and butter at bedtime to torment him, and he also mentioned the tiresome lack of variety in the menu at home. This led to Harry's acquiescence in Miss A's suggestion that she have a talk with his mother.

Unfortunately, the parents did not respond to requests to come to the hospital, and no home visit was made. The contacts of the social worker with Harry continued for about a year, and were gradually terminated because Miss A. felt that "the material he discussed seemed quite superficial, and the interviews served only to prolong an unprofitable dependency relationship."

The diagnostic problem posed by Harry's lack of conformity to his diabetic regimen cannot be considered solely as an individual matter, but is closely connected with our knowledge of normal adolescence, and of the frequent disturbance of adjustment to authority at this period. Was Harry's breaking of his regimen an example of a normal testing of authority at adolescence? The medical history showed that there had never been a good control of his disease, so it was certain that no foundation had been laid for good dietary habits in his earlier years. Just how capable is a boy of fourteen of taking responsibility for his own health regimen when it involves deprivation, and being different from other boys? Should the medical worker center efforts on him or on his family? One is mindful that fourteen is an age of "becoming," and one wants to build toward more responsibility in the future, while being quite aware that a boy cannot take more than his previous years have prepared him to assume. A good contact with the family, and a good life history would seem essential for understanding this boy's difficulties.

Miss A. felt that interviews with Harry would bring out his emotional problems, apparently connected somehow with his rivalry with his brother, Mike. She was disappointed that continued interviews did not bring out much more than the first—a liking for Mike, and use of him to take Harry's part with the mother, at the same time that he felt that Mike was the favored one. From the experience we have in social living, we wonder how we could expect a boy of fourteen, whose normal emotional expression is through action, to give increasingly detailed and interesting accounts of his inner emotional life. We also wonder whether the emotional dependence which the worker felt was "unprofitable" was not an important diagnostic clue to Harry's need for a friendly relationship with someone. The history of Harry's infancy was not obtained until long after the first social service contact was over, although the general family picture had been known in the clinic. Harry was the oldest of six, and when he was born his mother had been in bed with a heart condition and felt frightened and helpless, giving much of the care of the baby to her husband. The birth of other children followed when Harry was three, four, five, eight and twelve. While Harry was still fed by a formula, the doctor had wanted his parents to enter him in a baby contest, and had prescribed a large amount of Karo syrup to make him fat. When the parents decided to stop this exhibition of their child, a diet heavy in sugar was rather suddenly taken away from him. When Mike, born when Harry was four, developed a skin affection as an infant his screams were so disturbing to the neighbors that his mother often held him in her arms all night. Mike was put on a diet which did him no good. Finally the parents disregarded his diet and he recovered through use of a patent remedy. When Harry was five, and while his mother was in the hospital giving birth to her fourth child, he developed diabetes in an acute form. When Harry was six, his father began to be ill with the chronic progressive disease, multiple sclerosis, which finally made him unable to work, after nine years of effort to hold a job.

Two and a half years after Harry's first contact with social service, he was referred again for the same problem, and an interview with Mr. Wicks was held at his home. This visit brought out a number of significant things about the family life. The cheerless poverty of the home was obvious, as was also a strong family feeling. The boys had worked after school ever since they were old enough to do anything, selling papers, doing school janitor work, or whatever they could get. Harry had done well in school, in spite of his heavy outside schedule and fluctuating health. The mother had gone to work in a restaurant when Mothers' Assistance was refused because of a medical disagreement over the extent of Mr. Wicks' disability. It was only in the period of this visit that the situation was eased somewhat for the family by acceptance of their application for Mothers' Assistance. The reason the overburdened parents had not responded to invitations to come to the clinic was now clear.

The attitudes of the family toward Harry came out in interviews with both father and mother. Like the other children, Harry was counted an asset for his earnings, and was described as a "good guy," though he was exasperating because of his squabbles with the younger children. The mother spoke of the burden his disease was to her, correcting herself to say, "I mean to him, of course." The father called him a "weakling," and spoke proudly of the next younger boy who was "normal." The father was eager to talk of what the loss of his own powers meant to him, and of how he now could be of scarcely any help around the house. He spoke feelingly of how wonderful his wife's care of him had been.

This information clarified, though belatedly, the diagnostic question whether the casework focus could be upon Harry, to make him the responsible factor in carrying out his treatment. Here was a youngster, deprived almost from birth of satisfaction of the normal need to be loved and cared for. At the time when his sense of being loved would come most from being fed, he was first stuffed with sugar and then deprived of it. He suffered loss of attention at the birth of younger children, who came in rapid succession. The dramatic illness of Mike, occurring soon after Harry was four, must have impressed him greatly, and diet must have been much discussed in the family—to the disparagement of keeping a diet. Through the years when his mother was giving much of her affection to her sick husband, life was saying loudly to Harry, "You have to be sick to be loved and cared for." As he grew toward adolescence, when a boy normally identifies himself, if he can, with his father, Harry's model of manhood was a father going down the slope toward certain death. There is some evidence in the interview held with the father that he identified Harry with himself, and gave him sympathy for his weaknesses rather than expecting him to free himself from his disability.

With all of this history in mind, the question whether it was indicated to direct treatment toward making Harry completely responsible for keeping his diabetic regimen translates itself into, Can this boy, severely deprived throughout his whole life, voluntarily *deprive himself*, as his medical treatment demands? Posed in this form, the question points to a search for satisfactions, for incentives for living (instead of dying like his father), and for strengths to reinforce the strengths that Harry had shown. He had managed to make a success of his school work, to be a part-time wage earner, and to maintain a normal interest in sports, all despite a severe health disability.

Looking back to the beginning of contact, the casework indications were for a whole-family approach to this problem. Undoubtedly, the caseworker would have had to go to the home when the family, overburdened as they were, did not come to the hospital. A rigid adherence to a rule that people must come to the office sometimes robs casework of an essential diagnostic opportunity. If the father, who was apparently the more mature parent, could have been reached when Harry was fourteen, his disease was less advanced and he might have been able to give a good deal of personal attention to Harry. Perhaps he could have broken his own identification of Harry's illness with weakness (as he showed signs of doing in the one interview that was held with him later), and could have made him feel that healthy living was worth the trouble it took. Harry's mother could perhaps have been helped to change her "keeping after" Harry from nagging to the minimal, but essential, support of his wavering resolution. Could there perhaps have been some enrichment of living for the whole family, to relieve a bit their turning upon each other in irritation? All this would be difficult, burdened as they were with many demands on their time and strength, but when was the ingenuity of good casework easy? By whatever means, the casework treatment of an extremely deprived individual must relate him, somehow, to resources in his social group and in the community, and to a search for satisfactions to strengthen him, before he can meet successfully deprivations which may be inherent in his disease or his life situation. That he needs to be stronger to meet, or to change, conditions of deprivation, is a challenge to a caseworker to find solid nourishment in the essentials of living for him, somewhere.

7.   Diagnosis and Reality

The fallacy in these three case examples lies in the assumption that emotions are separate from what happens to a person in daily living, something packed away in the unconscious, which must be "released," after which the person will have peace of mind, and can solve his own problems. Going a step further, some theories of casework assume that helping with practical problems is a kind of benevolent insult to the client's capacity for self-determination, constituting interference with his own way of doing things, and, if this succeeds, making the client "dependent." Back of all this is a philosophy which makes the *idea*, the person's feeling, the really primary factor in adjustment to living. By this philosophy, not fully conscious to most social workers who act upon it, poverty, sickness and friction in social relationships become problems because of conflicts within the person, and can be overcome if he is freed from his entanglements with unconscious desires which cannot be satisfied in reality. This concept assumes that reality factors are not the province of social casework, but that the client, freed by treatment from his unconscious blockings, will then make his own adjustment to them. Reality, however, includes such facts as inescapable poverty, incurable illness and social relationships made impossibly bad sometimes, not by the client but by others over whom he has no control. Preoccupation with his unconscious conflict may have no effect on these conditions, nor may the person ever become a standard-type mature adult, as a result of bringing all these conflicts to consciousness. His capacity to deal with external realities may be nonexistent or range up to adequate, depending on what his whole life experience has taught him, and the kind of person his original endowment plus that experience has made of him. Diagnosis consists in seeing the person *in* his reality, and in his active efforts to deal with it.

The scientific base for a profession like social work, engaged in helping people to live, cannot make ideas and emotions the primary reality. Like science in other forms of contact with the real world, a science of human adjustment has to take what it finds by experience to be true, and deal with this reality as experience shows to be necessary. Social work has fallen into confusion because it has tried to make itself a profession on an idealistic, instead of a scientific approach to reality. It has tried to deny incurable poverty, illness and social maladjustment, first by assuming that the solution lies in treatment of unconscious conflict within the person, instead of in society itself. Then, in self-protection, social agencies have moved away from contact with cases in which poverty, illness and friction were too obviously beyond the reach of a change in the client's feelings. Refusing such cases, agencies often said to the personal service workers at the Maritime Union who referred them, "This is not a case for us. It has too many reality problems."

Coming back to our question, Is diagnosis an imposition? the answer is yes if the so-called diagnosis ignores the objective reality with which the person is struggling, and from which his emotional conflicts are, at least in part, derived. This is not really a diagnosis at all, but an added burden put in the way of the person's solving his own problem. A diagnosis which is really a "seeing through" (in which the professional person usually leads because of special experience and trained skills, but in which the client shares continuously his own indispensable knowledge of his needs and resources) is a distinctive service of professional social work. Such a penetrating social appraisal requires much ability to use psychiatric knowledge about personality, but to use it in a dynamic way. The important question is not what a person has packed away in his unconscious (as if it were a storehouse), but how he is using the interplay of forces in his mental life to cope with the objective world around him.

Perhaps we could sum up with a working definition of social casework:

> Social casework helps people to test and understand their reality, physical, social and emotional, and to mobilize resources within themselves and in their physical and social environment to meet their reality or change it.

v i i. Who Hath Despised the Day of Small Things?

1. Why Study Short and Minor Services?

Is it possible to reach an idea of what social casework is which is not limited to the brand name of particular schools, and which squares with the best that we know about human relationships in social living? That is a much more important question than whether the personal service department at the National Maritime Union Hall, which responded to the needs of the users of the service was, or was not, doing professional social casework. It is important for thousands of people working in social agencies to have some measure for their own activity and growth. Thousands of public assistance workers, many medical social workers in hospitals with large intake, workers in short-contact agencies like Travelers' Aid and Red Cross are told, and believe, that they cannot, in their setting, really do casework. They are discouraged from taking professional courses because they see no way of using the casework which is often taught, and which is equated with solving emotional problems through a series of interviews in a protected setting and process. Some of them who do a fine, sensitive job with people are made to feel, whether or not they have had graduate school training, that while they have a gift for the work, they should never aspire to the title of professional unless they can do "intensive" therapy or consultation on emotional problems.

The explorations we have made have suggested certain criteria for a quality of work with people which is different enough from the good offices, or the kindly meddling, of unskilled friends to be called professional. These criteria include a background in the social sciences such that one can know people and situations with real competence. They include a scientific attitude, that is, respect for facts and willingness to search for them whether or not they support personal bias or wish. They include an ability to create a relationship of life-giving quality, free from need to punish or protect, stimulating to the client's own activity and growth.

We are about to study two examples of what we mean by social casework, in somewhat more detail than those given in previous chapters in illustration of a single point. These two are chosen, as were most of the others, from the experience of the personal service department of the National Maritime Union, not only because the writer can give them with more vividness for knowing the agency, but because that department became a social laboratory in which the caseworkers were close enough to the clients to observe, more easily than in the usual social agency, their reactions to the methods used. The seamen, who were the articulate public of the department, were free to say what they thought, and to help the caseworkers to test their methods against the realities of living.

The examples chosen began with simple requests for information. One was a single interview; the other consisted of two appointments within less than a week's time. There was no demand on the part of the case-worker for more contacts than the client would seek. From the initial request, in both cases, stemmed a search for the most significant among many relevant factors which made up the problem. An attempt was made to see the problem, not as a mass of trouble impossible to handle but as something which could be broken up into its component parts, of which at least one could be worked with by the client himself. The caseworker was consciously giving support and stimulation as she saw the need for each, helping the client to go out and begin to work on his problem in daily living. It is in living that problems are normally solved, with professional skill to aid at points where the person finds himself so enmeshed in the web of difficulties, and his own reactions to them, that he cannot find his way.

Not one but both of these men were sick enough emotionally to need psychiatric treatment. One could not get it at all, and the other could not reach it without casework help. Each had immediate problems to solve which involved his own action, and in which casework, not psychiatry, was the appropriate professional assistance. Fortunately for these men, the caseworker did not try to give them psychotherapy, though in each case she was a qualified psychiatric social worker. Instead, she used psychiatric knowledge in the simplest decisions, and in services which would seem to an uninitiated observer to be just the most natural thing to do. She drew out of social casework the rich possibilities which are so often unseen and neglected.

While it is never possible to show exactly how a thing is done, the detailed comments are intended to make the thinking behind the process as clear as it can be made. If these two illustrations show how the simplest service is not too small to demand the best in professional skill, they will have served their purpose.

2. The Man Who Lost His Grip

It was a painful story which came from the lips of Edward Grier, a tall, graying man of fifty who took his turn at the reception desk, trembling with emotion. He asked where he could find a good lawyer. The receptionist for the day, a skilled caseworker, knew that the name of a lawyer was not enough, even if she could have given it. She made an appointment for him to see a caseworker in her office in a few minutes. She passed on to Miss W., who was to see him, the following: "Brother Grier has a marital problem which troubles him deeply. Lest he may focus it differently than he has with me, I am sending you my impression that he needs to talk over something else more than the legal side of his difficulty."

It was a little startling to Miss W. to have Mr. Grier sit down at her desk, a gentleman in his whole appearance and bearing, and use a vile race epithet toward the man who had stolen his wife's affections. He knew that his union was strong in condemnation of such a term, and mumbled an apology. Miss W. noted, but did not show that she heard the expression. (Later, Miss W. learned that he had done the same at the reception desk. He had also told his story in much the same way there, as if he had rehearsed it over and over.) Mr. Grier went on rapidly to say he had to "wash a lot of dirty linen."

The story started as he gave identifying information:

"My address? 10 Goddard Street. That was my home for seventeen years until yesterday when I moved out bag and baggage. I was a prisoner of war in a Jap prison camp for four years. When I came back, I did not blame my wife too much. This fellow, Pete, a seaman too, and an old friend who had boarded with us for years, had kept coming there between trips. A woman is left alone and you can't cut her off like a slice of bread. I could forgive what had happened if it had stopped there. I didn't dream she would keep on with Pete behind my back. It is two and a half years since I came home, and only lately I found out about his letters addressed to 'darling', and written as if they were man and wife. When he came into port on the Gulf he wrote her every day. I protested. Finally, she broke down and asked for her freedom. She did not want to leave. It was her home, she said, though I had spent nearly $2,000 refurnishing it after I returned. She said *I* should leave. She said I could not keep her from seeing Pete. I did not want our daughter who is fourteen to know. I call her Baby. I planned my leaving when Baby was going to camp for three weeks, and her mother had gone to see her off."

Much of the bitterness of the story came in the recital of his attempts to get legal advice. At the Domestic Relations Court, he was told there was nothing he could do to force his wife to give the man up, unless by prosecution for a criminal offense, which he realized would hurt Baby terribly, and do no good. When he said, "My God! It is intolerable to live with such a situation," the social worker said to him, "Why don't *you* leave? You are a seaman and it is more natural for you."

At the office of the Assistant District Attorney he got the same advice. The precinct police told him they could not interfere unless there was a scene of violence. He was so desperate, lying at his wife's side and knowing he had lost her, that he thought how it would feel to strangle her. Then he thought of Baby, and the destruction of his own life, and thought the price of revenge was too high.

At this point, Miss W. saw a need for one or two questions to focus the problem. She had missed any mention of the solution the wife had asked for, divorce. She said:

> "I do not know what your religious beliefs are, or how you feel about divorce. Was that considered, or is it out?"

He said, "I am a Catholic." Then he trailed off into vague remarks which indicated to Miss W. that he might have considerable conflict in that area.

She asked if he had talked this over with his priest.

He had not mentioned it to Miss W., but, yes, he had. The Church's stand on divorce had been explained to him. Miss W., not wanting him to linger over something he could not deal with, and wishing only to let him know she understood, said, "As I understand it, the Church recognizes what your wife has done as sin, but can not legalize a sin."

He agreed. The conclusion of his talk with his priest had been that Father Dubois would talk with Mrs.

Grier. Mr. Grier was sure his wife would not talk with the priest.

COMMENT: At this point, Miss W. saw urgent need of "first aid," if the interview was not to degenerate into despair. She must get the man able to be a man, at least, before it was possible for him to be active in doing something positive with his life. So far, he had only restrained his hatred, and his impulses to destroy, and had taken himself out of the situation on the basis of advice which had cut his self-respect to the quick. It was as if the Law and the Church sided with the guilty parties against him. He was to take all the loss, silently, or it would be worse for him and those he loved.

Miss W. asked why he thought the Court social worker and the Assistant District Attorney had not suggested divorce, with provision for maintaining his rights under the law. She answered this by connecting their attitudes with that of the Church. They were not choosing to insult him, and throw out his rights as of no importance. They were community agencies which could not advocate a course not sanctioned by his church. Mr. Grier's mood lightened almost perceptibly. "Of course. I see that."

COMMENT: This placed his problem back with his conscience, and brought him up to his need to know what he really wanted to do, or could do. He did not mention divorce again, and Miss W. was not sure which of three hypotheses was nearest the truth (or all of them blended). 1. That his religion settled the whole question for him. 2. That he still had conflict which he repressed because he could not deal with it. 3. That denial of his wife's request for divorce was a form of revenge which he need not feel guilty about. These matters were not part of the caseworker's job at this point. The emphasis must be placed on the problems he could deal with.

The next step was to find the focus around which Mr. Grier could do something positive. Miss W. said:

"I suppose that what concerns you most in all this is what your relation to your daughter is going to be. Is it your wish to take her out of her mother's custody and make a home for her?"

He said he knew that would not be possible. Mother and daughter are so close they are "intertwined like two rose bushes." (Is the symbol significant? Thorns for him, as well as beauty?) It would kill them both to be separated. They could hardly bear the three weeks of Baby's being away at camp.

COMMENT: Was this another dead-end for his hopes? What could he possibly find that would give him status and meaning in his daughter's life?

Miss W. began to talk about how important to any girl of fourteen her father is, important to her growth into a woman. She said she had worked with children in child guidance clinics (to put this bit of general orientation on a scientific, not sentimental basis), and a clinic would say that it would be of the greatest value to Baby if she need not feel that she had lost her father at this time. How well had they known each other prior to the fateful four years when he was a prisoner?

He said he had either worked ashore or made short trips during most of his daughter's life. They had been fairly close. Miss W. asked if he could perhaps set up a home somewhere, maybe with friends, where it would be perfectly proper for a young girl to visit for a week or two during his shore vacations. He thought at once of a home of "friends of ours" where he was sure her mother would agree to Baby's going.

Then he brought out another problem which he had repressed before. The Assistant District Attorney had told him his daughter was already exposed to immoral influences, and perhaps the Children's Protective Society could take her away from her mother for moral neglect. His conflict over this went deep. Was he wronging the girl to leave her, or would he be revengeful and destructive if he tried to take her away?

Miss W. asked what he thought Baby's feelings were about Pete. He quoted what she said after he had told her mother to pack Pete's belongings to send to him, and to write him not to come there after the next voyage. Baby said, "Daddy, I know I shouldn't say this, but why are you sending Uncle Pete away? I love Uncle Pete, and Mother does too, and he is a good man."

COMMENT: Miss W. saw that Mr. Grier was confused by a conflict of moral admonitions which were anything but clean-cut, and too abstract to be applied in an actual situation. What looked like scruples for his daughter might be revenge. He could not be sure what was best for her future. He lacked essential information about the psychology of children of fourteen, with which to make a decision.

Miss W. again began to speak about emotional growth and discussed how children, as they grow up, leave behind the belief that their parents can do no wrong. They have to learn that parents may even "sin," and yet can be understood for what they are, and still cared for affectionately. Mr. Grier agreed that while it is impossible to tell just how much Baby knows, or is disturbed about the sex relationship, she evidently still needs both her mother and "Uncle Pete." It is her father, Miss W. said, whom she needs most of all, especially if she is confused about her other relationships. Could he help her by being someone she could turn to, whose love would be steady and unfailing?

Mr. Grier was evidently not able to promise very much just now, but he became clearer than he had been before that it would be very destructive to drag the girl from the only home she has known, and force her to undergo Court proceedings to prove her mother unfit. Naturally, these would rob her of her affection for her father also. Her mother would only carry on a still more hypocritical role which would be even more unwholesome for her daughter. He seemed relieved, as he talked, and more able to do what he could do for his daughter without conflict. He came to regard the Assistant District Attorney's opinion as little better than his own ideas of revenge.

Since he was in a seamen's agency, it was natural to ask him how satisfying his job is. Miss W. had noted, but did not comment on, his rating as a messman, relatively an unimportant job for a man of his age and evident ability. She wondered in her own mind if he had a health difficulty, after the malnutrition and horror of prison camp, which may have unfitted him for more responsible work on a ship. To get some idea of what his work meant to him was to round out an impression of what he had to work with in rebuilding his life.

Mr. Grier said that, like many seamen, he had wanted to give up going to sea, but when he had made a new start in the Navy Yard, after his return from prison camp, he was laid off in a postwar retrenchment, and could hardly make a living except at sea. He had nothing just now to make him want to stay ashore.

Mr. Grier came back to his original question, but this time it was transposed to whether he needed legal advice. Certain indications for it, such as divorce, or a Court battle to remove the child, were eliminated by his analysis of the situation. Was there any need for protection of his right to his daughter? Miss W. could not answer that, and perhaps, now that he knew better what he wanted to do, it might ease his mind to review the legal aspects with a lawyer. He thought it would. He knew the Union attorney, and thought the latter might suggest names of reliable lawyers specializing in domestic relations cases.

At the end, Mr. Grier reviewed his own course at points where he most blamed himself. Why did he let this go on so long? Why did he not tell Pete, after his own return, that he wanted the home for the three of them? He, of course, trusted his wife not to carry on the relationship secretly. Then Pete made a gesture of getting married. Mr. Grier told his wife that it was a gesture of frustration, but he gave Pete $200 for a wedding gift. Then the wedding never came off. After that, Pete wrote how lonely he was on shore leaves, and Mr. Grier let him come back. He seemed to be trying to build up his respect for himself. Could he think of himself as better than a fool?

He emphasized that he would arrange support for his daughter. He had left $200 for the house, and had left his slippers there, so no one could say he had deserted. As he rose to go, he said it helped to talk things over.

DISCUSSION: Whatever we suspect of deep psychosexual difficulties (which may have been induced by this man's experiences as a prisoner of war, and may have antedated them), one fact determines the appropriateness of his being treated by the methods of social casework rather than psychotherapy at the time of this interview. His pain, and his sense of loss of manhood were so great that he could not have asked for anything at the moment except some minor practical service. To suggest psychotherapy at such a crisis would be to drive deeper the stab that life had given him, that *he* was inadequate to hold his place as a man. He would need building up before he could deal with what might be true in that area. In the meantime, he had just a little area in which he was forced to take some position, and confused about what to do—the situation itself. That is the field of social casework—a person-in-a-situation.

Mr. Grier's experience with social agencies he consulted had been frustrating and bitter. Perhaps he could not have gone anywhere else except to his Union which he trusted not to hurt him. Was it significant that twice, on the threshhold of the interview, he went through a gesture which seemed compulsive, to use an epithet for which he would be most abhorred, and then quickly to apologize for it. Was this a sign of the terrific repression of his hatred of Pete (there were no threats at any time against him), which broke through for one instant where he hoped he dared to be himself, but where he expected his "dirty linen" to be unacceptable. Was it the compulsion to know the worst, "Will you too reject me?"

If a problem as deep as this is to be dealt with in a

short-contact agency, it is essential not to minimize for a moment its seriousness, and not to be diverted by the simple request, but to move rapidly toward certain objectives:

1. A working understanding of the situation, gained by listening to the spontaneous story of the client. There may be much detail or very little, all of it having some meaning to him or it would not be associated with his account of his trouble. The skilled caseworker is listening with the question, What is his unconscious, as well as his conscious, mind trying to tell me? The language may be full of symbols (like the slice of bread and the rose bushes, and others less obvious). The story, which might be starkly, "I rage, I hate," will be told in terms more acceptable to the conscience of the speaker and the supposed standards of the listener. Through it all, the caseworker follows the thread of what seems most significant to the problem with which the person is grappling. When questions are asked it is to fill gaps in essential knowledge of events and relationships. As important as the problem is the kind of person who is dealing with it, what his strengths are as well as his handicaps.

2. Development of a relationship with the caseworker, which is the dynamic of professional help. We can explain its use only by borrowing terms, such as saying that the caseworker is like the catalytic agent in a chemical solution, making reactions occur between compounds that would re-

main inert without its presence. We see the effect of a helpful relationship in simplest terms when we say that sharing a burden lightens the load, or that talking over a painful experience with someone we trust enables us to say about it things we had not been able to say before, even to ourselves. The psychological explanation, by the theory of repression, is that the mind represses what it can not deal with, or what is too painful to be borne. The individual is then left without use of his conscious intelligence, in respect to that matter, and is released to use his intelligence again when a relationship with a person he trusts gives him confidence and security enough to face the difficulty, and to try to think it through with the other's support and help. Such a relationship frees the person not only to understand more about his difficulty, but to begin to act upon his understanding. This kind of relationship is frequently found in social living, but more reliably in a professional person who is trained, as in social casework, to an understanding and self-discipline which can make the most conscious and controlled use of relationship.

3. Supportive treatment. If in the process of understanding the person and his situation, the caseworker finds him in a state of shock, too prostrated to focus on the problem or to act, emotional "first aid" may be indicated. In this case, Miss W. had to counteract the devastating blow to Mr. Grier's sense of personal adequacy. He had to get back his self-respect before he could think of what he did or did not want to do in the situation. Miss W.

saw a need to make his hurt less *personal* (he thought he had been told that even guilty parties had more rights than he). She showed him how the position of the Catholic Church on divorce, which was in no way personal to him, influenced the advice he had been given, and his own estimate of what solutions were possible, or impossible, for him. This bit of treatment "generalized" the problem, and took much of the hurt out of it.

4. A focus on the part of the problem that the person can deal with. This focus is arrived at by an estimate both of what the problem contains, and of what the person is able to do. It sets in motion *activity,* which is a healing force as well as a direct means of solving the problem. In this interview there were so many negative and hopeless factors that it was hard to find one positive one for the man to take hold of. It might have been that his relationship to his daughter was hopeless too. Fortunately, there was something in that which could be cultivated, and Mr. Grier's essential sympathy for his wife (revealed in many of the words he used) made it seem that he could give his daughter something she needed without using her destructively to punish her mother.

5. Practical next steps. Having found the focus of the problem, what is to be done, and how, depends on what the person himself brings up, related specifically to the action he is contemplating. In Mr. Grier's case, it was probable that he would soon have to return to sea. He needed to go with

some peace of mind, and some ability to plan his next meeting with his daughter. In relation to that kind of movement, within himself as well as toward some relationship with his daughter and his wife, one can understand his reversion to questioning about his part in this whole affair. It was not so much a return to self-abasement, as freeing himself from feelings of self-distrust which would be impediments to taking up his life anew, and making something out of it.

6. Provision for future contacts. In many cases a definite time for return would be suggested, particularly if the caseworker foresaw that elaboration of what had been talked over would create new questions and fears with which the person would probably need help. In this setting, since the man would feel free to come at any time, it would be necessary only to make clear that Personal Service is open just for talking, and does not require that anyone have a specific request. If she felt that Mr. Grier might be vague concerning the kind of problems in which counsel could be of use, Miss W. might have indicated that parents of adolescent children often came to talk over something which puzzled them. This bit of focus might have helped him to come, and also might have been therapeutic in emphasizing to him that he *was* a parent, with all the responsibilities and satisfactions which that entails.

By way of showing how differently this case would have been approached under another theory of casework, we include here some notes of a confidential discussion of it with a representative of a family agency. The question asked was, If this man had come to your agency, how would you have handled the situation? The substance of the reply was this:

> "First of all, the man would have to define in what area he wanted our help. If he was just genuinely confused about what he wanted, it would not be our function to help him work out of his confusion.
>
> "We do not see it as our function to furnish a supportive relationship.
>
> "We would insist on seeing the daughter if he wanted to have our help."

The differences are obvious, but comment on certain points may make clearer the approach to social casework which we have been relating to social living:

1. Taking a person where he is means that if he needs help most before he can define his problem, that is where help should be given. Mr. Grier had already gone far in his analysis of what seemed to him an inescapable dilemma, and had shown great self-discipline in doing so, but had been blocked by his deep sense of rejection. (Some clients need much help before they can get as far as he had gone.) He could not have been told to go home and define what he wanted of the agency without another severe trauma. He had formulated (out of what experience he had) that he needed a lawyer. The formulation was inadequate (as the diagnostic insight of the receptionist

at Personal Service told her even without an interview), but it would not have helped the man to say, "We have no lawyers here" or "Think about it further." In this theory of casework, a formula is not important, for admission or otherwise, but it is very important that a troubled person have the experience of *finding* what he wants. He can then formulate what it is important to him to state as a guide to action.

2. The use of supportive treatment has already been noted. It often makes the difference between a person's being blocked or able to proceed. The interview at Personal Service was deliberately handled so as to convey to the man that his reserves would be respected, his pain would not be probed, his strength would be found for him (in case he thought he had lost it) and built up toward finding what he wanted and what he could do. This was just something of professional skill added to what we know as the best in social relationships.

3. The use of diagnosis is apparent in the Personal Service method of helping. The suggestion for a goal, a relationship to his daughter in which he could be helpful to her, came directly out of what was found in the situation. It could not have been formulated beforehand, as a rule of procedure. To have, on the other hand, a rule that a caseworker must see the daughter, in such a situation as this, would be to ignore the principle that diagnosis precedes action. Needless to say, a rigid procedure would have been destructive in this case. The

theoretical basis for it, that the girl must have suffered a severe trauma, and would need psychiatric
help contains assumptions which would be highly
questionable in social living: For instance, that
psychiatric help is a panacea, without regard to
what it does to relationships within the family
group, or within the person who may not be prepared for it. Or, that the caseworker cannot trust
the father to give his daughter what she needs,
or to ask for help when he has been made aware
that it exists. To Mr. Grier, of course, this would be
still another trauma.

4. The Personal Service conception of social casework did not place the problem automatically as
within the person's emotional life, to the exclusion
of social factors which had a great deal to do with
his emotions. In Mr. Grier's case, it was quite true
that he may have had serious psychosexual difficulties which may have contributed to the situation in which he found himself. However, he
could not grapple with a neurosis, dating either
from childhood or from prison camp, without
psychiatric help which was not available to him.
He had to earn his living at sea, and could not earn
enough, even if he were ashore, to pay for psychiatric treatment, or to take time out to attend a
clinic if there were one with time to give him. He
had to deal with the part of his problem he could
reach, and that was something in the social situation which was positive, his relationship to his
daughter. The caseworker had to increase, not

impair in any way, the capacity he had to do something with it.

3.   Youth Seeking Guidance

Ben Land, a fine looking, sad-faced young man, was not quite twenty years old when he came to the personal service department of the National Maritime Union after a telephone referral from the consultation service of a private social agency. He was not a stranger, since he had made loans there two years before, but he was reluctant to come because, as he said, he had given his history to five social workers in the last week, and did not feel like going over it again.

He came because he wanted psychiatric treatment. He was not eligible for a free clinic because he had a thousand dollars saved, but he was afraid of the high fees he had heard psychiatrists charged. The social worker at the consultation service said his Union Personal Service might be able to arrange for treatment for less, and he thought Personal Service might have information about benefits under a "seamen's bill of rights." He was not sure he was eligible to consult Personal Service anyway, because he had retired his union book several times, and was not at this moment a member. In explanation of his uncertain status as a seaman, he said that he was not satisfied either ashore or at sea, but he had read a book by Sandor Lorand, and got the idea that his case might not be hopeless because of his heredity, as he had always supposed. "Environment is more important." Apparently he only dreaded being questioned, for he told his story spontaneously, and with evident relief in talking.

His mother went insane when he was nine. He does not remember much about her, except that she frothed at the mouth. A relative took him away the day she went to the State Hospital, where she still is. He said his father ought to be there too. Ben lives with his father, but, "I only sleep there." His father used to beat him, but hasn't since he went into the Merchant Marine when he was sixteen. His childhood was unhappy. The relative with whom he lived for awhile accused him of making his mother insane, and said, "I'll kill you before I'll let you make my wife insane." Then he was in a congregate home for orphans until he went to sea. He had a nerve-wracking time during the war, and has a Certificate of Continuous Service for sailing the required number of months in the Merchant Marine. He does not think war service made him sick. "I was always maladjusted."

Ben began his search for help by looking up his old social worker at the Home. The social worker thought he was vocationally misplaced, and should finish high school, and then make a new start. Ben was advised to go to a Vocational Bureau, which told him his intelligence was normal, "good enough for college, but not for postgraduate work." He wanted more definite advice, and was referred to another counseling service for more tests, from which he has not had a report. By this time, however, he was sure he could not succeed in any vocation until he had had psychiatric help. He was sent to a private family agency which sent him to the consultation service which sent him to the Union.

It was evident to Miss S., the Personal Service caseworker, that Ben was under great pressure of anxiety, as the referring social worker had said, and should be gotten to a psychiatrist immediately. The only hope of an early appointment was with a psychiatrist in private practice. Ben agreed to pay the fee for an initial series of diagnostic interviews, and to discuss with the psychiatrist the estimated cost of the treatment he would need. The doctor could advise him whether he would be able to combine treatment with a job. His jobs ashore have been on addressograph work, and he has never kept one more than a week or two. Miss S. had confirmed with the referring agency that they could not go on with social service interviews in conjunction with psychiatric treatment, but that they hoped Personal Service could be the base for any social adjustments needed. While, technically, Ben was not a union member, it was possible to be flexible where no financial aid was involved, and to give needed service until his relationship with a psychiatrist was established. Miss S. was able to make an appointment for him for that same evening with a psychiatrist who understood seamen's problems. Her handling of the referral, with a brief summary of the life situation given over the telephone while Ben listened, was designed to make an interview with a psychiatrist seem not too formidable. The life history, which he had written out and had left at the Consultation Service, he could pick up and take with him to the psychiatrist. He seemed incredulous when he was told that the seamen's bill of rights had not been passed, and thought he must have *some* benefits for his war service in the Merchant Marine.

In the next two days, Ben showed his anxiety by coming to Personal Service twice, at times, as it happened, when Miss S. was out, to ask if the psychiatrist whom he was seeing each evening was really a good doctor.

He was also almost obsessively insistent that he must have benefits to cover psychiatric treatments, and when he remained unconvinced about the seamen's bill of rights, was given a referral to the Union's research department to look up the facts for himself. The case-worker whom he saw at the reception desk talked with him enough to give him some outlet for his anxiety, and suggested that he bring his questions on his next appointment with Miss S. Ben said he had arranged with the doctor to pay a fee of $10 an hour for four or five interviews, and after that the fee for further inter-views could be adjusted. Ben appreciated the doctor's explaining "his position" to him. He did not want any special favors, but was fankly worried that he would "go broke" before the treatment was finished. On the third day from his first visit, Ben came with a critical problem. Quoting from the record:

"In by appointment. Says his father opposed his taking treatment and seized his bankbook. He tried to explain, but Father wouldn't listen. When he told Father he wanted to avoid getting sick like his mother, Father got very excited, and said all he needed was a good beating. Ben said that didn't help when he was a child, and Father insisted it did. Ben asked if Father wants him to leave. Father said no, he was still his father, and Ben could stay. It was his home. Ben says actually his father needs him when he gets sick, and Ben feels some obligation to stay, though he himself would get well faster almost anywhere else. Also, he has no money. He has not told his father he quit his job last Monday, and when Father asked him how much visits to the doctor cost he lied and said $3. Even that sum made his father wild. He thinks doctors only take your money to enrich themselves. It was then Father took the bankbook, and Ben could not get it back except by force. Now, Father has put it in his safety deposit box.

"Ben has borrowed from a friend the money for his next appointment with the doctor. At first he thought he did not want to ask his father to go with him to the doctor, as it would waste his $10, but then he thought it was necessary to try it in order to persuade his father to let him have treatment. If that fails, he will have to go to sea, and earn enough to pay for some treatment. His own estimate of his future, if he does not have help, is that he will either go insane like his mother, or go to sea and become a chronic alcoholic.

"In spite of his fear and agitation (shown by trembling lip, and biting at his fingers), Ben shows a strong purpose to try to get well. He did not mention the seamen's bill of rights this time. He did ask to be reassured that the psychiatrist is a good doctor."

COMMENT: So far, the casework treatment had been much like a business relationship, illuminated, it is true, by Miss S's psychiatric training which made her aware how disturbed Ben was, and how quickly one must work to get him to a psychiatrist. The professional relationship must have been such as to give him confidence and overcome his reluctance to go into his story. It brought him back when he had been twice disappointed in not finding Miss S. in the office, although his referral to a doctor had been completed. Miss S. had asked no questions, except about practical details needed for getting him an appointment with the psychiatrist. Now there was a social problem on which he needed help, for his money was suddenly gone, and the treatment into which he had already put much effort was imperiled.

Miss S. answered Ben's question about the doctor by going over with him again what psychiatric treatment involves. She assured him about the doctor's standing and professional integrity, and showed why costs are so high because of the time spent in psychiatric treatment. She prepared him for the possibility that he might need some time to get better, but could say to him that if health was important to him there could be no better investment of his savings, and he could count on the doctor's making it no more costly than was necessary. She helped him get a better idea of the way the patient's cooperation assists psychiatric treatment. Then she focused on the problem at home in this way:

> "You are sure you want treatment, and you are willing to spend a reasonable amount of your money (if you can get the use of it) to invest in better health. How can you get your father to let you have your money? Can we see why he acts the way he does? What has his life been like?"

Ben gave the following picture of his father: He comes from an orthodox Polish-Jewish background, and is so fanatically religious that he spends all his time praying, except what is necessary to do his simple housework, and to earn his living as a night baker. After his wife went to the mental hospital, he "got all his affection from God" and gave none to his children. The older son and daughter remained with him. Both have now married, and the father feels that he has lost them both. Because the son asked him for money to start a little business after he came out of the army, the father says children only care about what they can get out of you. Ben said he himself spent his money wastefully when he first went into the Merchant Marine, but his father should realize that he got over that, or he would never have saved a thousand dollars.

Miss S. asked about his father's having relatives in Poland. She said how terrible it was to bear what had happened to the Jewish people, especially if it was one's own relatives who were murdered. She talked about how younger people try to forget or take comfort in other ways. Ben himself had controlled his nervousness at times by plunging into the work of the Union's political action committee. Religion is an old and well-tried way.

Ben returned with Miss S. to a discussion of what he could do. He said, "You know I see my father differently, somehow. Not just crazy." Maybe it would be worthwhile to try again to persuade him to accompany Ben to the psychiatrist, or at least to this office. Ben said at first he was afraid to try it. He could not trust himself when his father would "start raving." He might even hit his father, and that would not be right. Miss S. thought we might think of some way to make it easier, rather than tackling the thing cold. Would a letter from Personal Service strengthen his case? To show him what was meant, and also to give Ben a dif-

ferent picture of himself than he might have seen reflected in his father's eyes, she began, with Ben's help,
to compose a letter:

> "Dear Mr. Land,
>   We are writing you to say that we know your
> son as a responsible member of this union, of
> whom we are proud, and for whom we hope a suc-
> cessful and happy future."

That first sentence was to meet the father's fear that
his son was a silly child who would be taken in by a
quack doctor. They discussed whether it would be
best to put the need for treatment on the ground of
avoiding the fate of his mother. Ben agreed with Miss
S's estimate that his father's fear of mental disease was
probably so great that it would seem fantastic to him
to think that talking to a doctor could avert the inevitable tragedy. It was agreed that the vocational approach would be better. The letter went on to say that
many young men had great difficulty after the war in
finding what was the right work for them. Many became very nervous with worry over it. There was every
reason to believe that Ben could be helped to decide
wisely, and to build up his health, by seeing a doctor
whom we could recommend. The cost would be limited
to what he could afford, and the doctor, or Personal
Service at the Union would be glad to give Mr. Land
any information he might want.

Ben brought up several difficulties connected with
sending the letter to his father if it was written in English. He reads only Yiddish, and would go to some of
his cronies for a translation which would be certain to
be garbled. Miss S. said there was a possibility that we

could get the letter translated into Yiddish, and that if his father came in we could arrange to have a Yiddish-speaking caseworker see him. Time was saved for an appointment for Mr. Land on Monday, when that caseworker would be sure to be in. By this time, Ben thought he could try to handle the interview with his father without the letter, and could still have the visit to the office or the letter as resources in case he had trouble.

On Monday, Ben came in jubilant. His talk with his father changed Mr. Land's attitude so that he gave back the bankbook. Now Ben will go ahead with the diagnostic interviews with the psychiatrist, and try to work out a plan of treatment that his father will not oppose.

DISCUSSION: Some theories of social casework would classify the help given to Ben Land as a minor service facilitating medical care. Some would see that the change in the boy's attitudes toward his father and himself required skill and the use of a professional relationship, but would still see the service as minor unless the caseworker was the psychotherapist who worked with Ben toward a reorientation of his emotional life. Supposedly, some agencies would estimate Ben's state of anxiety as serious enough to indicate immediate referral to a psychiatrist, and others would undertake work with him without seeing any risks in it. Such is the confusion in the field of social casework that many agencies would not see the possibility that they might safely work with a fairly sick person *in a casework way,* around a practical problem which the client could work on, while it would be definitely dangerous for them to use their interviewing techniques to bring to

the person's consciousness emotional material which
neither they nor he could deal with.

The important consideration, in decisions about what
a social agency shall take on, is that Nature's provision
for protection through the mechanism of repression is
for survival, and is to be respected. Repression is not
just a device to give interesting exercise to psychothera-
pists in breaking it down.

The writer will never forget a case in which a
woman who had gone home from a mental hospital
after a depression was treated by a caseworker in a
family agency through weeks of interviews which drew
emotional material from the unconscious until the patient took an overdose of sleeping pills left on a table
by her bed. The presence of mind of her twelve-year-
old daughter saved the patient's life, but a child should
not have had to deal with a situation which would have
been guarded against if someone who understood depressions *practically* had taken a responsible part in the
aftercare. While one could not say that the interviews
produced the impulse to take too heavy a dose of pills,
the psychological probability is great that they contributed to it, as the pressure on the conscious adjust-
ing mechanism, faced with formerly repressed material,
became increasingly intolerable.

While Ben Land's caseworker was relieved of responsibility for psychotherapy by referral to a psychiatrist, her way of working with Ben would in any
case have been around whatever practical problem
there was in the situation. She might have had to give
emotional first-aid, as in the Edward Grier case, but of
a sort that would meet the needs of the unconscious
without dangerous release of repressed material. Such

needs as feeling accepted, feeling as adequate as
most people, seeing some hope of gaining love and recognition in one's natural setting are like basic needs for
fresh air and rest and simple food and drink in cases
of physical exhaustion, and it is only the exceptional
case in which any one of these is contra-indicated.

Ben Land's attitudes were changed in the process of
doing something about his situation, with the caseworker whose understanding of it, and of him, made
her able to initiate the activity and to draw him into it.
She trusted him, and made him able to trust himself
and his father. Was the writing of a letter which was not
even used a wasted effort, or a minor service? Did it
take less of skill, or give the caseworker a less satisfying
opportunity, just because the service was all that Ben
required at the moment?

VIII. Whose Need and Whose Responsibility?

1. By Way of Review

These explorations in the philosophy and practice of social work have been a trail-blazing venture, indicative only of how much needs to be done before our theory and practice are integrated, and both represent a philosophy of human relationships which we can stand by with conviction.

To review our course up to this point: We have studied an unusual experiment, a social agency working in a membership organization, not with the idea that conditions there could be transferred to social agencies in general, but that we might learn from this, and from scrutiny of everyday living, how people give and take help most naturally.

We found certain conditions essential: Help must be connected with increase, not diminution, of self-respect, and it must imply the possibility of a reciprocal relationship of sharing, within a group to which both giver and recipient belong.

We did not find these essential conditions always present in the membership organization, in daily life, or in social agencies, and we did find much confusion and maladjustment over the giving and taking of help. It will not solve the problem of the resistance which social agencies meet in clients to know that one of the sources of it is a sense of not belonging among the people who think of themselves as "the community." To recognize that fact, however, is to save ourselves from seeking the whole trouble in the unconscious mind of the client, or believing that to have a problem which makes help necessary is inevitably a shameful experience.

We have explored certain aspects of our practice which give us perennial concern. These are: Whom shall we help (if not everybody), when and how much shall we give (whether of material benefits or services), and how shall we find the real problem and help the person in trouble to do something about it. Again, we do not have answers, but we have been testing methods of making real in practice what we believe about people.

What *do* we believe? The premise with which we set out found social work to be an inseparable part of the society in which it grows. Our practice has its roots and finds its opportunity in the kind of concern for the well-being of people which society really has. What we social workers believe about people, then, cannot be uninfluenced by what society wants of us. Neither can the philosophy we hold and the practice of social work in our hands fail to make an imprint upon the society of our time. For this reason, what we believe and do in our profession is of great importance, not only for the growth of our profession in the future but because there is no more critical question in the world today than the relation of all nations to the well-being of their people.

2.   Society in Conflict

Our approach to the question of society's responsibility
for what happens to people will naturally be from the
point of view of our own profession. Social work does
not express a unified conception, in our society, about
how to deal with human need, but rather reflects sharply
contradictory attitudes. For instance, while there is a
growing acceptance of public responsibility for meeting the subsistence needs of the unemployed, in a
period in which unemployment is a chronic problem,
relief standards are being attacked and driven down-
ward to the point that relief is only slower starvation.
Work relief, which might be so used as to maintain morale and conserve workers' skills during a period
of depression, is made in some communities an excuse
to cut down employment of other workers at normal
wages. In this way society as a whole cancels out its
own assumption of responsibility for meeting human
need.

We have noted that private social agencies are prevented from being the "sensitive antennae" of the community, searching out unmet needs, because they must
trim their work to what it is wise to spend, out of funds
whose limits are set without relation to the extent or the
kind of need.

We observe that welfare legislation, which we regard
as preventive of much of the human misery with which
we deal, is opposed by organized and well-financed
lobbies and propaganda agencies. Nothing could be
more obvious than the need for a Federal low-cost
housing program, but real estate interests block the
necessary legislation year after year, while destruction

of family life goes on, in dwellings unfit for human habitation. Medical care is so costly and so ill-distributed that thousands die and many more are disabled for lack of it every year, yet even medical societies levy assessments on their members to lobby against an adequate Health Act. It is needless to multiply examples, for we see them every day, and experience them ourselves in the prices we pay and the protection we go without.

It looks as if the great undertaking which we call social work is reflecting both society's concern for people in need and the wish of powerful groups to profit by such conditions as an acute shortage of houses or a surplus of unemployed labor. We have noted that the interests which oppose really constructive social work constitute only a small minority of the whole population, but influence a much larger sector through their ownership of newspaper chains and control of radio broadcasting. Many hard-working folk who sincerely want people in trouble to have a fair break are frightened by propaganda to the effect that the country is being ruined by taxes to support a "welfare state," and that people on relief are "chiselers" and social workers "sob-sisters." Social workers know that it is not the small percentage of the national budget which goes for schools, hospitals and social services which should give us concern, but why it is that a hundred times as much goes for military expenditures which ultimately mean destruction of human life.

The fact which confronts us when we look at social work in all its aspects is that opposition to welfare measures, and to good social work generally, is not a cultural lag in community understanding which we can remove by doing a good job, and interpreting it well. Social work can defend its standards only if it realizes the organized nature of the opposition to it, why these interests are opposed, and where its own allies are to be found. It is the purpose of this concluding chapter to explore further the question of its title, *Whose Need And Whose Responsibility?* We shall use two examples to pose the question concretely:

3. Finding the Question in a Community Center

The following experience in organizing a neighborhood Community Center taught its sponsors a great deal.

The community, a fast-growing section of a large city, lying between an industrial area and suburban towns farther out, was divided by a boulevard which created a "this side and that side" like the traditional railroad tracks. On one side lived people who had many cultural advantages, even though the mothers often had to take jobs to provide them for their children. On the other, the population was less predominantly composed of white collar workers. Families were large, and the wage earners were principally industrial workers. The community had grown too fast to be normally supplied with play space, or public meeting rooms.

The group concerned in sponsoring a Community Center included civic leaders from both sides of the boulevard, professional people, representatives of small stores, and of labor unions. The sponsors were conscious that they had personal interests which led them to give their time and what money they could raise to the project. They wanted the Center not only for social enjoyment but to develop a more healthy and active sense of citizenship. They were worried about juvenile delinquency, which they thought of as largely localized on the disadvantaged side of the boulevard. Merchants wanted to check vandalism. Everyone deplored recent outbreaks of violence against Jewish stores, which, though they might be instigated by depraved adults, threatened to involve teen-age youngsters.

The Center was started with enthusiasm, and enough financial backing to provide comfortable quarters in the shopping center serving both sides of the boulevard, and to secure the services of a trained group worker and a part-time janitor.

The children who lived near flocked to the Center for after-school fun for which they had had no place but the streets. They came particularly from the "disadvantaged" side of the boulevard, and to them dancing and music and craft activities were endlessly enticing. Their parents who had not been able to provide such things, and who were perhaps a little doubtful about their value, held aloof, waiting to see why such an opportunity was being offered, but willing for their children to enjoy it. The children on the other side of the community had more play space around their homes, and had had, and outgrown, many of the simple activities which the Center could offer. They were therefore less eager in the use of its facilities.

A year later, when the expenses of the venture had outrun its resources, a meeting of the board of directors was called to consider how part, at least, of the program could go on. They hoped that some organization could take over the rooms (which included an assembly hall and space for several groups of ten or fifteen), and could run a program with volunteers without too great cost. An interchange of opinion between two members of the board expresses the kernel of a difficulty which had been present from the beginning, but never before so clearly shown.

A businessman spoke first, one who had acted as treasurer and business adviser of the project:

> "I want to see this go on. Don't misunderstand me. There is nothing in it for me, personally. I don't need it for recreation, and my family get their culture and fun in other ways. But I think the project is needed in this community, and I will do all I can to support it."

A representative of a labor union answered, with a good deal of controlled emotion breaking through in his voice:

> "I am not like you. I do not support this for somebody else. We working people are not used to having anything handed to us. If we want something we work hard for it, we clean the building, we take turns being here to look after the kids. It does matter to us whether our children have a place to play, and a chance to learn good things. We are ready to put in real work to have something here that we can use."

Here are indicated two attitudes toward a social welfare project, attitudes which are different in quality. One is that supporting a project is doing something for somebody else; the other that we are doing something for ourselves. To put it another way, the businessman is saying, "I do not need but I give." The workingman's statement, including the emotion with which he spoke, added up to this: "We do not want charity from those who do not need this project, but what we need we will work hard to provide for ourselves."

In the end, the Center had to be given up. The two attitudes expressed at the board meeting were carried over into the evaluation which the different groups set upon the outcome. From most of the sponsoring committee, of whom the businessman was the spokesman, came expressions of regret, and the remark, "It is too bad that the community was not ready to support a project as worthwhile as this." The members who saw the service as something they wanted for themselves simply added this to other things they wanted and could not afford, such as better housing, better health care, and so on. It is not on record that anyone questioned whether their taxes should have given them more city services in this rapidly growing community. They were accustomed to going without, and other problems of making ends meet were very pressing.

Those of the sponsors who had put a good deal of themselves into the Center had much to ponder over as they reviewed its history. They had not thought of themselves as being philanthropic, but just being good neighbors, and using intelligence about it. They belonged, all of them, to the community, and came from both sides of the boulevard, though predominantly from the more comfortable people. It had not occurred to them that the factor of a more privileged group doing something for people less privileged would operate in such a setting. Yet, when it came to feeling a personal need for the project, those who really wanted it most could not afford it, and those who had been most influential in starting the Center gave it up with as much relief as regret. They had begun to feel the burden of giving to support something which their children did not need in just that form. The statement of the labor representative on the board, "I am not like you" was a rather shocking reminder that class differences might exist even in a neighborhood project like this.

4.   "We Are Responsible"

Take another example, this time from the USS-NMU joint project. One administrative question could never be settled to the satisfaction of both parties. United Seamen's Service wanted to consider its staff group in the NMU Hall as it did any other unit of its personal service department. It had placed them there simply to give service to seamen, who happened to be members of that union, in the place most convenient for them while they were obliged to be in the hall waiting for shipping assignments.

The National Maritime Union, however, could not sponsor a "foreign body" in its hall. It could not consider any service to its members divorced from the responsibility of the members for it. The Union insisted that the final word as to policies must come from the membership, through their elected officials. There were democratic ways of holding those officials accountable, procedures for appeal and review of decisions in membership meetings, council meetings, and the biennial convention. They were glad to cooperate with another agency serving seamen, but they could not surrender control to it.

We have seen that some social workers, looking at the project from the outside, questioned whether professional people could work ethically in a setting in which they were subject to another organization. Those who served in the project learned to feel the difference between taking their direction, as to policies, from a board composed of people in different circumstances from the clients, and finding their clients a part of the directing group. The startling difference came in the degree to which the seamen thought of the service as theirs. Social workers who had never had clients who approached an agency with that feeling now sensed that their work could indeed be closer to the people served when these also took responsibility for its policies.

To put their discovery another way: These social workers had been taught to adapt their work to the community in which it is done. Now they found a community of men employed in one industry, who asked only the same flexibility of them. This time, however, it was a community in which there were no great differences of income or status, and in which common interests had welded the members into an organizational instrument for active improvement of their condition. It was the most natural thing in the world for them to take responsibility for any service which their union set up in its hall.

5. How Active May a Client Be?

Returning to discussion of the practice of social work in social agencies, our profession has grown away from the tradition of doing *for* people to that of helping them to solve their own problems. Are we, however, entirely freed from the wish for their dependence which is embodied in the choice of the word *client* to represent those whom we serve? A client was, in Roman history, one of the dependents of a patrician family who turned to it for protection and guidance. When we reflect the contradictory attitudes of our society toward people in need, do we reflect both the wish, on the part of the majority of people who are struggling themselves, that misfortune should not "get a person down," and the fear, on the part of a comfortable and powerful minority, that the underprivileged will not be "kept in their place?" This conflict of attitudes is symbolically expressed in the institution of social work itself. Need is supposed to be in one part of the population, and responsibility for meeting need is assumed by another part on its own terms. We have seen that this contradiction is as present in public social work as in private. While funds come from taxes of all groups, it is the large property interests with strong legislative influence who determine on what standard public services shall be supported.

This basic fact about social work, its divided allegiance, has been an ever-present problem in all these studies. In social living, people share resources within their family, neighborhood and interest groups, in which all are potentially both givers and takers. Is it inevitable that the small groups in which sharing is taken for granted must remain isolated examples of a healthy kind of mutual helpfulness, while whole communities and units of government operate social services on a different principle: the "haves" giving to the "have nots," but taking away from them, at the same time, their right to have any responsible voice about the services they use?

We discussed in Chapter III the role of social casework in a public assistance agency, as a counter-force to the deterioration of relief recipients which results when administration of relief is regarded as merely a distributive and police function. Seeing the applicants as individuals, understanding their living situation, adapting what may be done under the law to their specific needs, going beyond just keeping them alive to building up their own personal and social resources—this is what makes out of an otherwise inhuman routine a professional service.

To get the opportunity to give that kind of service, public social workers have to have strong backing from citizens in the community. To fight the interests that would make subhuman creatures out of people to whom industry has denied jobs, the public welfare services must have especially the backing of two groups of citizens: First, those who are now forced to live on relief, or are very close to needing it. Theirs is no academic interest in relief standards, but a real struggle for survival. Second, those who have organized themselves into labor unions to keep a decent standard of living for their families if they can.

There is a closer connection between the interests of these two groups than either has seemed to realize. Where there is no standard of relief that approaches decency, there is no floor below which wages may not be forced. People will take any work to live, and force out decently paid labor. Conversely, where there is a strong labor movement it is not possible for communities to set relief expenditures at the lowest point.

When we social workers think of helping clients to be active we generally have in mind such a sheltered workshop as a man's own personality, or his family relationships. He struggles with his contradictory impulses, or learns how to deal with his mother-in-law constructively. We shrink from picturing, even, the client who might try to do something as a citizen of his community. Probably our habit of individualizing makes us see him as battling alone, against overwhelming odds, and we are moved to ask him where in his unconscious he gets that hero stuff.

The theme of this book is not individual displays, even of courage which is sorely needed in our day, but social living. Social work, we feel, ought somehow to lead to more social approaches to solving problems that beset individuals and families. Clients (despite the history of the word) will feel themselves *belonging* to the community only when they take part in a real effort of the plain people to see that their social services are truly social and really serve.

6. Social Workers Are People Too

Our explorations have faced us with a choice between contradictory forces in our society: those which are moving toward the welfare of the people, as the people's own concern and responsibility, and those which destroy human life in preventable misery and war, and relieve poverty only grudgingly to keep the privileged position they hold. Organized social work, reflecting this contradiction, might give us an illusion that we can both help people and keep them passively dependent. Actually, there is no middle road for us. Our profession has advanced enough for us to know that such help is no help at all in any professional definition, but destroys the priceless freedom to be a man or woman of full stature. The resistance we meet is one measure of our clients' will to take responsibility even in circumstances which seem to defeat them. Especially when we think people are expressing to us their wish to be passive and dependent do we have to be professionally alert to know whether they are really saying that life has denied them the essentials, and the unessentials we offer may as well be as we wish.

The real choice before us as social workers is whether *we* are to be passive or active. Shall we let the existing forms of social work, full of contradictions as they are, shape us to their mold? Shall we let customs which may have prevailed in our agencies for so long that nobody thinks about them any more determine our practice? Shall we be content to give with one hand and withhold with the other, to build up and tear down at the same time the strength of a person's life? Or shall we become conscious of our own part in making a profession which will stand forthrightly for human well-being, including the right to be an active citizen?

We are, most of us, the readers of this book, employees of social agencies whose policies we feel we do not have much part in making. We are subject to the same insecurities which beset the people we serve, insecurities differing only in degree from theirs. We are fellow citizens, all wanting a better life for our communities. There is every reason for us at least to work with our fellow citizens as with our own. They are not an alien group to us, however much they may have been made to feel so in their community. We cannot accept society's attempts to segregate Negro people from white, Jewish people from Gentile, foreign-born from native-born. They are all our own people. We cannot accept denial of civil rights to any because of nationality, creed, color or political belief. If we did we would be accepting a denial of full manhood, when professionally we claim to be working to develop full manhood.

What are we to do to carry out our professional responsible in a society which (an influential part of it) denies the basic human rights which are the foundation of any attempt to do professional work with people? We must, first of all, know that we have allies. The great majority of the people of America are with us in wanting a good life for *all* people. If they seem full of hate and prejudice they are most probably the victims of hysterical fear which does not belong in their lives nor correspond with their interests. The trade unions which have made real gains for all their members have been those which saw the absolute community of interest of workers of all colors and creeds and have walked right over prejudice to victory.

We social workers have professional organizations to defend standards. We must make them effective. We have unions in social work to defend our right, as workers, to conditions in which we can do work of high quality. In using the organizations we have we shall find others in the community also fighting in organized ways for the same issues in human welfare.

In living as social beings, we shall find the enrichment of our professional work and the clarity of purpose that shall make one whole of what we think and what we do. This book is dedicated to an unbreakable tie with the interests of humanity.

DATE DUE